*The Nightingale in
the Garden of Love*

T0294340

The Nightingale in the Garden of Love

~

The Poems of Hazret-i Pīr-i Üftāde

Paul Ballanfat

Translated from the French by
Angela Culme-Seymour

ANQA PUBLISHING • OXFORD

Published by Anqa Publishing
PO Box 1178
Oxford OX2 8YS, UK
www.ibn-arabi.com

© Paul Ballanfat, 2005
© English translation, Anqa Publishing, 2005
Translated from the French by Angela Culme-Seymour

First published as *Hazret-i Pîr-i Uftâde: Le Dîvân*,
by Paul Ballanfat, 2001, Les Deux Océans, Paris

This edition published 2005 by Anqa Publishing

A CIP catalogue record for this book is available
from the British Library

ISBN 0 9534513 8 0

Printed in Great Britain by
www.biddles.co.uk

CONTENTS

v

Contents

Contents

THE TRANSLATORS

Paul Ballanfat studied Philosophy and Islamic Studies as well as Arabic, Turkish and Persian, and currently teaches at the Jean Moulin University at Lyon, France, where he is head of the Department of Turco-Persian Studies. Paul has concentrated on Sufism in Persian and Turkish culture, and is the author of several books in French, including translations of Rūzbehān Baqlī Shīrāzī's *The Spirits' Procession* and *The Unveiling of Secrets*, and Najm al-dīn Kubrā's *The Blossoming of Beauty and the Scents of Majesty*.

Angela Culme-Seymour is Honorary President of the Muhyiddin Ibn 'Arabi Society. She lives in Scotland. Angela's translations from French include Ibn 'Arabī's *Fusūs al-hikam* (published as *The Wisdom of the Prophets*) and 'Abd al-Karīm al-Jīlī's *Al-insān al-kāmil* (published as *Universal Man*).

ACKNOWLEDGEMENTS

We would particularly like to thank Aliyyah Robertson for helping with the English, Emel Soylu for her invaluable help and expertise in checking the English translation against the original Turkish, Lulu Villiers-Stuart for the watercolour painting on the cover, and John Brass for the calligraphy on page 89.

The calligraphy reads *lā illāha illā hū*, which may be translated as "There is no god but He".

The photograph on the back cover is a view of Üftāde's house and the dervish lodge where he taught (see page 45). The minaret of the adjoining mosque is visible above the roof.

TRANSLITERATION

The Poems of Üftāde were originally written in Ottoman Turkish, which utilised an Arabic script with some modifications. Today the Turks use the Latin alphabet, to which they add certain special letters in order to convey the full range of Turkish phonemes. To give a clearer idea of the pronunciation of people's names and technical terms, we have transliterated these characters as follows:

c = j (as in **j**ump)
ç = ch (as in **ch**eer)
ğ = not pronounced except as a glottal stop
h = always aspirated (as in **h**ome)
ş = sh (as in fi**sh**)
ā = long a (as in c**a**rd)
ı = [i without a dot] short e (as in fath**er**)
ī = long i (as in s**ee**)
ö = ir (as in b**ir**d)
ü = French u (as in **r**ue)
ū = long u (as in b**oo**t)

PREFACE

This book is a translation of a collection of poems by one of the great masters representing Ottoman Sufism at the height of the Empire. This collection has been the subject of several publications, first in Arabic characters and then more recently in Latin characters under the careful eye of Mustafa Bahadiroğlu.[1]

Üftāde was not, strictly speaking, a mystical poet like Yunus Emre or Niyazi Misri. He was first and formost a spiritual master, founder of one of the great Ottoman brotherhoods (*tarikat*). His poems reflect, above all, his interior state and his advice to his disciples. They also have a ritual function, and have certainly been sung since his time in his dervish lodge (*tekke*), where the practice of audible invocation and songs took place, but not dancing, in contrast to other brotherhoods.[2]

In spite of the profound admiration that he had for the *Mathnawī* of Rūmī, founder of the Order of the whirling dervishes, he is not connected to the line of Persian mystical poetry. His poetry is simple, and is closer to Turkish Anatolian mystical poetry, whose great exponent was Yunus Emre. His poems belong in the category of those brotherhoods which often used to compose *ilāhīs*, that is to say, religious songs that accompany ceremonies of collective invocation. A certain number of them are still sung today, and they have

---

1. The Ottoman edition dates back to 1328/1910 and was edited by Bursalı Tahir Effendi in Istanbul. Mustafa Bahadiroğlu has provided two current editions of Üftāde's *dīvān*, both published in Bursa: the first in 1995, including a long study of the master, entitled *Celvetiyye'nin piri Hz. Üftāde ve dīvān'ı*, and the second, abridged in 2000, entitled *Üftāde dīvānı*.

2. Üftāde explains that dance and songs are used to chase away conscious thoughts, but that the invocation of the formula of Unity, which is his way, is more effective, *Wāqi'āt*, fo. 114a.

given rise to old musical compositions in different styles. It was to be the same for his favourite disciple, ʿAzīz Mahmūd Hüdāyī, who would also write down a collection of poems, and these poems were used in the ceremonies and lodges in the master's line. One of these poems, which Hüdāyī composed in honour of Üftāde, is very well-known and sung in the brotherhood.

> The nightingale in the garden of love, Hazret-i Üftāde is …
> The doctor of the lovesick, Hazret-i Üftāde is …
> Perfect, arrived at the realisation of the essential Unity,
> the guide who holds the hand of the Friend, Hazret-i Üftāde is …
> Whoever seeks help for his soul shall reach his goal,
> the one who dissolves all difficulties, Hazret-i Üftāde is …
> Spiritual guide they call him, so seize the hem of his robe;
> the one who shows the Way, Hazret-i Üftāde is …
> Hüdāyī, be forever a sincere slave at his threshold;
> Know the truth: the pole of poles, Hazret-i Üftāde is …[3]

3. This poem composed by Mahmūd Hüdāyī about his master Üftāde serves as a religious song in several dervish orders. A very beautiful recording of it exists on the CD (track 15) accompanying Kudsi Ergüner's book, *La fontaine de la séparation*, Paris, 2000.

INTRODUCTION

Hazret-i Pīr-i Üftāde

Mehmed Muhyiddīn Üftāde (895–988/1490–1580) was one of the greatest figures of Ottoman Sufism. If he exercised a lasting influence over the Ottoman Empire, it is not due to his works. These amount to poems, which were gathered into a divan and have been translated here, and a collection of sermons that have remained unfound. One enormous work, compiled by his most important disciple, 'Azīz Mahmūd Hüdāyī (948–1038/1541–1628),[1] whose dervish lodge and mausoleum can be found in the Üsküdar area of Istanbul, shows the position occupied by Üftāde. This major work, entitled *Wāqi'āt-i Üftāde* ("Spiritual teachings of Üftāde") and written in Arabic, is a near-daily journal of the spiritual education which the master gave to his disciple, and is certainly one of the most important testimonies of Sufi education in terms of actual experience.[2] The *Wāqi'āt* is also the best document that we possess on the master's teaching, testifying to his deep insight, his profound knowledge of the spiritual Path and his metaphysical predilection, in particular his attachment to the doctrine of the Unity of Existence developed by the successors and commentators of the work of the Shaykh al-Akbar, Ibn 'Arabī (560–638/1165–1240).

1. For a discussion of his date of birth, possibly pre-948, his place of birth and his life, see the work of Hasan Kāmil Yılmaz, *Azīz Mahmūd Hüdāyī ve Celvetiyye tarikatı*, Istanbul, 1982, pp. 39ff.

2. We possess some copies of this work, usually called *Wāqi'āt-i Üftāde*, including a manuscript in Hüdāyī's own hand, Haci Selimağa no: 250, in two volumes. For the other manuscripts see *Azīz Mahmūd Hüdāyī ve Celvetiyye tarikatı*, pp. 114–15. Mustafa Bahadiroğlu and I are preparing the critical edition.

One of the major features that make Üftāde one of the greatest representatives of Ottoman Sufism is the fact that he is the founder of the Celvetiyye order, which like many others has disappeared due to the Turkish Republic. Decree 677 ordered the closing of the Sufi lodges and mausoleums on the 30 November 1925, launching a great wave of repression against Sufism, comparable to that which rained down on the dervish lodges and all Sufi practices of the fifteenth and seventeenth centuries under the name of the Kadizadeli movement, whose originators were deeply influenced by the writings of Ibn Taymiyya, and who had many masters executed and lodges closed down.[3] One cannot fail to notice an extraordinary convergence between the supporters of the secular republic and the religious *integristes* (fundamentalists) of the time, whom today we would call Islamists, united by the same hostility towards the body and spirit. So the Celvetiyye order disappeared like others, although some of them have been able to hide secretly until our time, with the last masters to direct the principal Celveti lodges being: Muhtar Efendi for Üftāde's lodge in Bursa, Mehmet Şemseddīn Efendi (d.1936) for that of Ismail Hakkı in Bursa, and Mehmet Gülşen Efendi (d.1923).[4]

The life of Mehmed Muhyiddīn Üftāde

Üftāde is the name by which Mehmed is usually known. In fact, it designates a surname that was revealed during a vision, following an episode which was to mark the path of his future life. Üftāde is a Persian word meaning "fallen", "perished", "ruined". The story of the way in which he adopted the surname is celebrated. It is told

3. See on this question the article by Ahmet Yaşar Ocak, "Oppositions to Sufism in the Ottoman Empire in the 15th and 16th Centuries", in *Islamic Mysticism Contested*, Leiden, 1999, pp. 603–13.

4. Mustafa Kara, *Bursa'da Tarikatlar ve Tekkeler*, Bursa, 1993, II, p. 134, and by the same author, *Tekkeler ve zaviyeler*, Istanbul, 1980, pp. 327ff.

by, amongst others, Ismail Hakkı Bursevī (d.1137/1724) one of the most illustrious Celveti masters, in his work on the spiritual line of the Celvetiyye.[5] In his youth, Mehmed had been chosen to perform the call to prayer in the Great Mosque of Bursa, the Ulucami, and in the mosque of Doğanbey, whose name is not specified. His call to prayer was so beautiful that people gathered to hear it and some fell into ecstasy, as he himself records.[6] One day he was offered a sum of money to compensate him for his service. But the same night Mehmed had a vision, during which it was said to him: "You have fallen (*üftāde*) from your station"; following which he immediately returned the money that he had imprudently accepted. It is thus that after having used the name Muhyiddīn, he abandoned it to use the name Üftāde.

This story was to have great importance in the care that he would take in future with money. In contrast to a large number of mystics living on gifts and other revenue taken from landed property granted by the State, as had become customary, Üftāde would always refuse such a gift. One story at the end of his life well illustrates this position of principle. The mother of Sultan Murad III (982–1004/1574–95), Nūr Bānū Sultān, had come to visit him and had brought a coffer full of money. Üftāde, as ever, would not accept it, but try as he might to turn down the gift, at the lady's insistence he ended up saying that she might leave the offering in a corner, where it remained untouched. One day, however, Üftāde exclaimed to himself: "Since this money arrived in our house, the blessing has gone. May it (the coffer) disappear!" and the coffer vanished at once. Then soon after Üftāde said: "They have driven away our Presence! Let us set off at once on our travels, let us not stay another instant!"[7]

Üftāde also gives advice to his disciples on the subject of money, when describing his attitude towards the salary he received as preacher in the Emīr Sultān mosque.

5. *Kitāb-ı silsile-yi shaykh-i Ismā'īl Haqqī bi-tarīq-i Jalwatiyya*, Istanbul, 1291, p. 78.
6. *Wāqi'āt*, fo. 14b.
7. *Menākıb-i Üftāde*, ed. A. Yunal, Bursa, 1996. p. 15.

I gave what I earned to the poor who searched for God, and I
distributed to each poor person two dirhams, on condition that
they would be content and would accept nothing from anyone
else. As for those amongst them who are not in need, let them
eat only by taking from their own lawful estate once each day
and night, and let them add nothing. Those that are in search
of God should accept nothing from the exterior, for that gets
in the way of handing oneself over in trust [to God]. As for the
lovers of God, let them eat what is lawful but twice a day.[8]

He himself recounts also how, later on, he came to resign from his
office of muezzin.

I became muezzin at a mosque, and for performing the call to
prayer I earned three dirhams, with which I paid the rent on
the house. One day I found myself flying close to the sky, and
saw men such as I had never seen here in this lower world. Some
said: "look at him, how he flies!" Others said: "If he didn't spend
sacred money, he would cross the sky." After that I abandoned
even the call to prayer.[9]

This story demonstrates the importance that Üftāde gave to the
relationship with money. Even lawful money could become a major
obstacle in spiritual realisation. There was for him a fundamental
incompatibility between religious duty, which can only be done for
God alone, and payment, which one expects. Spiritual realisation
enabled him to go beyond the apparent lawfulness of the act in order
to enter truly into the ethical sphere of freely given service and
handing oneself over in trust to God.

The story of the coffer is emblematic, mirroring in a certain way
Üftāde's spiritual life. It begins with him losing a spiritual station
which had been given to him by Divine Generosity, and then recov-
ering it, as demonstrated by the recollection of the fall and the rule

8. *Wāqi'āt*, fo. 38a. The work is full of advice and anecdotes to do with money
problems.
9. Ibid. fos. 37b–38a. See also *Menākıb*, p. 105.

which it brought. Then it closes with him accidentally breaching this rule, which was also to mark the end of Üftāde's life and his return to the world of pure spirits. These two stories frame the whole of Üftāde's spiritual life, and demonstrate the discipline which he put himself under. Üftāde, then, was one of those masters whose rule meant that one should renounce the good things of this world, and we may recall here the rule of Najm al-dīn Kubrā that one should renounce the two worlds to be counted amongst the men of God.[10]

Relations with those in power would also be founded on this principle. Thus, for instance, Sultan Suleyman the Magnificent (927–74/1520–66), having heard talk of Üftāde, invited him to his capital, Istanbul, and offered to give him two villages held in mortmain, which the master firmly refused. When the master and some of his disciples entered the audience-hall at the Palace, Suleyman the Magnificent received him by stepping down from his throne, taking seven steps towards him and asking him: "I expect something from you: that you accept us as a son", which the master accepted. After the dervishes had taken their leave, the Vizir Ibrāhīm Paşa asked how it was that the Sultan had shown such deference towards the master. He replied:

> He had behind him a lion which, had I not greeted him thus, would have swallowed me and my throne. One cannot compare him with other masters. The others want gold and money – they are on the way of the lower world. I wanted to make a donation of one or two villages to his dervish lodge. He formally forbade it.[11]

In return, Üftāde asked and got Sultan Suleyman to build a mosque at Hisār in place of a church which was next to his mausoleum.[12] At

---

10. See Najm al-dīn Kubrā, *Les éclosions de la beauté et les parfums de la majesté* (The Dawnings of Beauty and the scents of Majesty), Nîmes, 2001, pp. 10, 65.

11. *Menākıb*, pp. 111–12.

12. Ismail Hakkı, *Kitāb-ı silsile*, p. 79. Üftāde recounts that when the sultan's decree came, "I put a niche there in the direction of the qibla, we prayed inside and we preached there and performed the invocation of the formula of Unity for

a time when it was difficult to reject a king's wishes, Üftāde did not hesitate to refuse the gifts which were offered to him, as when Murad III wanted to make a gift to him of several places held in mortmain until finally, for the sake of peace and quiet, the master consented to receive some chestnut trees. This goodwill on the part of the sultans, from which Üftāde was able to benefit, reflects the marked taste which these rulers had for Sufism for a long time in the Ottoman Empire, despite hostility from religious scholars and fears that the brother-hoods were dominating social trends and politics in Anatolia.

A large number of brotherhoods were set up in the Ottoman Empire, especially during the fifteenth century, which saw the estab-lishment of the Kubrawiyye with Bukharī Emīr Sultān (d.833/1429), Sultan Bayezid I's son-in-law and highly venerated in Bursa; of the Suhrawardiyye by one of its branches, the Zeyniyye; of the Qādiriyye through the impetus given by Eşrefoğlu Rūmī (d.874/1469–70); of the Nakşbandiyye with Mollah Ilāhī (d.896/1491); and of the Bayrāmiyye with Haci Bayrām-i Velī (d.833/1430), disciple of one of the most famous saints of Bursa, Somuncu Baba (d.815/1412); not to mention the development of the oldest brotherhoods in Anatolia, such as the Mevleviyye or the Kāzerūniyye. The sultans, during the fifteenth century, consistently maintained relations with Sufi masters: one particularly striking example is Yıldırım Bayezid I, who was advised by his son-in-law and master of the Kubrawiyye, Emīr Sultān; Yıldırım was defeated at the Battle of Ankara on 20 July 1402 by Tamerlane – himself motivated by great respect for a certain kind of Sufism, and sufficient admirer of Ahmed Yesevī (d.562/1167) to have a mausoleum built for him, following a dream.[13]

The repression of Sufism began in the wake of Shaykh Bedred-din's revolt in Anatolia in the first quarter of the fifteenth century,

---

two years, before adding the stones to transform it into a mosque." *Wāqi'āt*, fo. 101b.

13. When Tamerlane fought Bayezid's troops, he recited seventy times a quatrain by Yesevī, reputed to help him overcome difficulties. See Fuad Köprülü, *Türk Edebyatı'nda Ilk Mutasavvıflar*, Ankara, 1984, 5th edn, p. 41.

and this was for political reasons, as power needed to be consolidated in Anatolia after the defeat by Tamerlane. But this opposition would become much stronger and more widespread in the following century, when many of the brotherhoods were attacked, and their masters executed along with their disciples, under the aggressive movement of religious scholars. This policy, coupled with serious political and social disorder, reached its peak in the reign of Suleyman the Magnificent. Religious scholars saw in Sufism the source of the decadence of Muslim society, and targeted those Sufi practices which could be most easily condemned, such as invocation, dance etc., thus reflecting the old distrust of religious rationalists towards outward manifestations of ecstasy. During this period some mystics even condemned a number of brotherhoods for heterodox tendencies that were too ostentatious and practices that were too eccentric. However, the influence of religious scholars on the sultans of the time was not so exclusive as it might at first appear from the executions, condemnations and closure of the dervish lodges. Moreover, religious scholars were not unanimous in their condemnation: some Şeyhülislām of the time, the highest religious authorities, were themselves affiliated to the brotherhoods; Zenbilli 'Alī Efendi (d.932/1526), disciple of the master Vefā of the Zeyniyye brotherhood, was one of these. Others changed their positions: Ibn Kemāl (d.940/1534), for example, who, after having been a powerful enemy of Sufi practices like dance, spiritual concert, veneration of a master etc, and having regarded those who engaged in them as outside Islam, ended up recognising the merit of the Halveti master, Ibrāhīm Gülşenī, became his disciple and was buried with a copy of the *Ma'nevī*, a mystical poem by the master 40,000 verses long.[14] Others were brought up in the Sufi way, like Ebüssuūd Efendi (d.982/1574) son of the Bayrāmiyye master, Muhyiddīn Yavsī (d.920/1514). Meanwhile, over-zealous authorities like Çivizāde Mehmed Efendi (d.954/1547) remained implacably hostile to the metaphysics of Sufism, and regarded the

14. Reşat Öngören, *Osmanlılar'da Tasavvuf: Anadolu'da Sūfīler Devlet ve Ulemā* (XVI.Yüzyıl) Istanbul, 2000, pp. 344–8, 369ff.

two most important exponents of Turkish Sufism, Ibn 'Arabī and Mevlānā Jalāl al-dīn Rūmī, as unbelievers.

In spite of the hostile attitude towards Sufism in the sixteenth century, the sultans felt sympathy and respect for the masters, and often became affiliated to one or many brotherhoods. Bayezid II (ruled 1481–1512), like his father, had great veneration for Emīr Sultān, the Kubrawi saint of Bursa, and performed an important pilgrimage to his tomb. He also maintained relations with several masters whose disciple he became, like Çelebi Halīfe (d.899/1494) of the Halvetiyye, or Muhyiddīn Yavsī of the Bayrāmiyye, whom he called "the Sultan's Master". Yavuz Sultan Selim (ruled 1512–20), who succeeded him, had as his teacher a Nakşbandi from Kastamonu, Halīm Çelebi (d.922/1516). He seems to have been affiliated to the Halveti master, Sünbül Efendi (d.936/1529), and to the Nakşbandi master, Muhammad Bedahşī (d.922/1516). According to Üftāde, Sultan Selim had a very special relationship with Ibn 'Arabī. The *Wāqi'āt* mentions several aspects of this:

> It is recounted that Sultan Selim went to see one of the enraptured saints, who was called Ak Bāzlı Baba, who said to him: "You will be Sultan, even though you will shed blood." When he conquered Damascus [Sept 1516], he ordered the Arabs to assemble near a rubbish dump which was to be found in the Salihiyya, and ordered them to empty and clear it. When they had cleaned it up, there appeared the tomb of Muhyiddīn Ibn al-'Arabī with the inscription Muhammad ibn 'Alī, and he had a cupola constructed above it.[15]

Another account describes the place that Ibn 'Arabī occupied in the sultan's interior life and the relation that he maintained with his own master:

---

15. *Wāqi'āt*, fo. 29a. For Ibn 'Arabī's influence on the Ottoman sultans and the role of Selim in the construction of the mosque close to Ibn 'Arabī's tomb, see S. Hirtenstein, *The Unlimited Mercifier*, Oxford, 1999, pp. 241–2. See also C. Addas, *Ibn 'Arabī and the Voyage Without Return*, Paris, 1996, pp. 7–8.

One day Sultan Selim said to his master Halīm Çelebi: "I saw in a dream that the saints of the Arab regions had gathered, and that Ibn ʿArabī was amongst them. They said: 'we will not give the land to Sultan Selim', but the greatest master opposed them, saying: 'We will give.' They came round to his view, and obeyed him." Then Halīm Çelebi said: "When you conquer these regions, have them construct a mausoleum and a collection of buildings", which the sultan promised to do and carried out.[16]

As we have seen, the *Menākıb* of Üftāde shows Suleyman the Magnificent, at his own request, receiving from the master a genuine spiritual education. He also had an affiliation to three other orders. After reading Rūmī's *Mathnawī*, he affiliated himself to the Mevleviyye, even taking part in sessions of spiritual concert, and dismissed the uncompromising Şeyhülislām, Çivizāde Mehmed Efendi, who considered Rūmī an unbeliever. Secondly, in his childhood he was initiated into the invocation and practices of the Nakşbandi order by Halīm Çelebi, whom his father put in charge of supervising his education. On his first journey to Belgrade he took with him a Nakşbandi master, Mehmed Nurullah Efendi (d.977/1569). Finally, he was also initiated into the Halveti order by two different masters, Nūreddīnzāde (d.981/1574) and Ibrāhīm Gülşenī, saying of the latter that "he has initiated me into a name, so that all that I ask for I obtain".[17] Similarly, we find Sultan Murad III secretly making visits to Üftāde in his dervish lodge.[18] The latter also encouraged the sultans in their struggle against the politics of the Safavids, who intended to spread Twelver Shiʿism to the detriment of Sunnism, and in the *Wāqiʿāt* he teaches ideas openly hostile to Shiʿism.[19]

16. *Wāqiʿāt*, fo. 8b.
17. Öngören, *Osmanlılar'da Tasavvuf*, pp. 245ff.
18. Ibid. pp. 183–4.
19. He accuses Shāh Ismāʿīl of spreading deviation and evil, of having been an innovator, by developing a school different from all the existing legal practices, and he asks God to protect the Muslims from Shīʿite beliefs. *Wāqiʿāt*, fo. 26a.

The birth of Üftāde

It is at the turn of this complex century that Üftāde was born, in the town of Bursa in 895/1490, in 'The Quarter of the Arabs' above the Inebey market where his father had come to live.[20] His father was originally from Manyas, and his mother from a little village near Bursa called Hamamlıkızık Köyü. His birth was surrounded by favourable omens. His mother dreamt that she saw her son dive into and come out of an ocean of milk, which his father interpreted as the announcement that his son would be called to become a perfect saint, who would be one of the people of knowledge and people of perfection;[21] this was characteristic of masters of the time, who received exoteric religious education before being initiated into mystical knowledge. According to Huseyn Vassāf, he was *Seyyid*, that is to say, a direct descendant of the Prophet. However, this descent may have been of a purely spiritual nature, coming through the devotion that Üftāde displays for the Prophet,[22] as we can see in this account taken from the *Menākıb*:

> Muhammad Çelebi recounts: "One day I was in the presence of my master, Mustafā Efendi (Üftāde's grandson). While he was talking, I was conscious of a perfume better than musk coming from the master. As I said to myself: 'What a wonderful scent', the master turned towards this poor person and smiled. It was

He also mentions a clearly anti-Shī'ite story about Muslihüddīn Efendi (ibid. fo. 82a).

20. For the dates of his birth, see Mustafa Bahadiroğlu, *Celvetiyye'nin piri Hz. Üftāde ve dīvān'ı*, Bursa, 1995, p. 45.

21. Ismail Hakkı, *Kitāb-ı silsile*, p. 77. Üftāde himself tells the story that his father had told him: "One day I woke up and your mother was crying. She told me: 'I dreamt that my son Muhammad was taken and put on a throne in the middle of an ocean of milk.' He said to her: 'Why cry when this is the good news that our son will be a person of knowledge?'" (*Wāqi'āt*, fo. 83a).

22. H. Vassāf, *Sefīne-i Evliyā*, Istanbul, 1999, II, p. 620; Yılmaz, *Azīz Mahmūd Hüdāyī ve Celvetiyye tarikatı*, p. 178.

clear that this scent came from his body. He said with joy: 'Last night in our interior world we kissed the blessed hand of Abū Bakr. This blessed perfume has come from his subtle body.' And he added: 'But if a privileged one amongst these creatures reaches the Muhammadian Reality, his body will be perfumed even better.'"[23]

Once Üftāde spoke of having a vision in which he saw that the world was "full of the Prophet's spirit, and that he heard and that he replied, and the one who is capable of hearing can hear him reply, and if there was no effusion coming from him, one could do nothing, neither talk to me nor listen to me."[24] In the same way, in a passage in the *Wāqi'āt*, Üftāde gives the rather ambiguous impression that he was in fact *Seyyid*: "In my early stages I wore a green coat. But one day it occurred to me that green was the colour of the clothes of the princes of the family of Muhammad. So I abandoned it out of regard for the clothing of my ancestor, and I chose not to use this colour except for the headgear (*tāj*)."[25] One source gives his father the title Shaykh 'Alī Efendi, but this is unlikely.[26]

Üftāde was very soon in contact with a dervish endowed with spiritual powers, who was responsible for leading the prayer and preaching in the mosque of Selcuk Hatun, Muslihüddīn Efendi as he himself called him. They very soon became like father and son. The sight of Muslihüddīn's spiritual perfection had a decisive effect upon the young Mehmed, who eventually begged his patron to accept him as disciple, asking him to lead him on the way of spiritual realisation. The master would not agree to this because of the young boy's

23. *Menākıb*, pp. 97–8. Üftāde explains that "the highest states and stations consist in being close to the Prophet" (*Wāqi'āt*, fo. 18b).

24. Ibid. fo. 39a.

25. Ibid. fo. 24b. The headgear, or to be more precise the crown, was a head-dress by which the orders were distinguished from one another, and a replica of which was placed on tombstones to identify the tombs of dervishes of such and such an order.

26. Bahadiroğlu, *Celvetiyye'nin piri Hz. Üftāde ve dīvān'ı*, p. 35.

age, and later, no doubt, because Üftāde was bound to his master
Hızır Dede. Üftāde must have been very impressed by this person,
whom he mentions several times in the *Wāqi'āt*, and he was clearly
still alive at the time when Üftāde was asked to preach in the Emīr
Sultān mosque, for he recounts how Muslihüddīn intervened to
persuade him to accept the job, as we will see later.[27] As Üftāde must
have started preaching between the ages of 40 and 48, Muslihüddīn
was evidently still living between 1530 and 1538. Üftāde describes
the virtues and spiritual training of Muslihüddīn in the *Wāqi'āt*.
His account shows a mystic who above all lets himself be guided
by his unveiling, and who does not waste the opportunity to go and
find what his visions show him, even when it involves those who are
named infidels.

> He used to say that he invoked the Unity of God night and
> day 70,000 times, and he possessed unveiling and spiritual
> powers. He told me that one day, during his retreat, it was said
> to him: "Go and see such and such a person in the church of
> the Patriarch of Constantinople." So I left the place where I was
> staying and went to this church. I asked for him amongst the
> infidels who were found there. They replied: "We do not know
> of him, but there is, over there in that cell, a man who hardly
> ever mixes with others." When I arrived at the door of the cell,
> this person came out. He said to me: "Come in, Muslihüddīn."
> I entered the cell and there I saw the signs of Islam. He told me
> to do my ablutions and he prayed with me. Then I wanted to
> take my leave of him, to go and eat something. I came on the
> day of 'Arafāt.[28] He asked me: "Are you in a state of ablution?"
> I replied "no" and he ordered me to ablute myself, which I did
> at once. He continued: "Shut your eyes, put your feet on mine
> and put your heart in confidence." So that is what I did. Then
> he seized me and drew me against his chest. We stayed like that

27. *Wāqi'āt*, fo. 82a.
28. A hill close to Mecca, where certain rituals are performed on the ninth
day of the month of pilgrimage.

for a moment and he said: "Open your eyes." I opened them and there we were at 'Arafāt. He said to me: "when you have finished your prayer, you will find me again here." Later, having done that which I had to do, I came back and found him where he had said. I again did what I had done the first time, and we found ourselves back in his cell. Some days later, I went back to see him, but I found his cell empty. I asked the infidels where he was, and they replied that he was dead and that they had buried him [in Christian earth]. I lamented, saying to myself that he must have been a demon. But then I saw him in a dream, and he said to me: "O Muslihüddīn, if you want to see me, come and join me on the tomb which is under such and such a tree in the Muslim cemetery." I woke up and went to the place he had indicated. Then he appeared to me as a Muslim, his face flooded with light. When I wanted to approach, he disappeared.[29]

Üftāde, in his childhood, was also in contact with another mystic, a dervish enraptured with God, by the name of Abdāl Mehmed, who also had a mausoleum.[30] The young Mehmed would also witness his unveiling and spiritual powers. Üftāde gives the following account according to the *Menākıb*:

I noticed each day that in the morning before the day rose, Abdāl Muhammad Efendi went to a large cave called the Cave of Cenk, in a place called Gökdere. He had long hair falling untidily from his head. Leaving his hair loose, he went up to the cave, stayed a moment, then came back down. One day, before he arrived, I rushed off to get there before him, I too letting loose my hair. As I let it loose, I saw all the kingdoms of the Arabs, the Persians, the Indians and the Europeans,

29. *Wāqi'āt*, fo. 38a. The same kind of spiritual power is reported with regard to Üftāde, who carries one of his dervishes in the same way as far as the new mosque of Kanūnī Süleymān in Istanbul, to perform the midday prayer there. *Menākıb*, p. 115.

30. This is a different person from the one mentioned in Mehmed Şemseddīn's *Yādigār-ı şemsī*, ed. M. Kara and K. Atlansoy, Bursa, 1997, pp. 269–70.

unveil themselves to me. No sooner had I covered my hair than
they vanished as if they had never existed. Then I saw Abdāl
Muhammad who had just arrived at the cave and who, seeing
me, took me by the hand and said to me: "Go Muhammad, off
you go, you insolent boy!", telling me off in order to get me to
go down. I kissed his blessed hand and went off.[31]

Üftāde may well have been impressed and felt great admiration
for these two people, but they were not his spiritual masters. As is
the case with other mystics, the choice of the spiritual life didn't
come about easily. Üftāde's spiritual aspiration was against his father's
wishes, who wanted him to have a career in the silk trade. We may
assume that Üftāde's father had been drawn to Bursa to work as a
silk merchant, since Bursa was a very important centre for the pro-
duction of silk. He had the trade taught to his son, who was then
compelled to do this work in spite of his repugnance for it, as he
himself records in the *Wāqi'āt*. Üftāde dreamt only of following in
the footsteps of the saintly people whose spiritual powers he saw,
even more so because he lived in a town where for a long time a
great number of dervishes had been coming – as we can see from
the number of lodges which the old sources record the existence of.
Eventually Üftāde could no longer tolerate the master with whom he
was serving his silk apprenticeship. More and more arguments arose.
One day, after one of these quarrels, he found himself in front of the
Great Mosque of Bursa – the Ulucami – and following a prayer, that
same night his employer died and his own father within the week.
Üftāde experienced these events as a real liberation, as he recounts
in the work of his disciple, 'Azīz Mahmūd Hüdāyī:

31. *Menākıb*, pp. 50–1. A variant of this story is mentioned, without the name
meczūb (the enraptured one) in which Üftāde contemplates "the totality of the
worlds, the light of the sun of divine secrets" and when the *meczūb* sees that, he
tells him: "Oh child of pure lineage, do not miss the rules of good education
– otherwise you will suffer and go astray" (ibid. p. 29).

My father entrusted me to a silk merchant, and I worked for
him for eight years despite the repugnance and aversion that
my heart experienced. One day I met my master in the Great
Mosque. He asked me if I was working and I replied: "Yes."
He continued: "Work, my son, and I shall bring you to a free
workshop!" My tongue let slip that God would not accept his
prayer, and yet my employer died that night and my father the
same week. Four of us were left, me, my brother, my sister and
my mother. We lived for a time, my mother working all night to
weave the silk and I following my trade. Then my brother died,
and my sister married a man who agreed that my mother could
live with them. Thus I found myself alone, enjoying my tran-
quillity, and I could dedicate myself to the spiritual life under
my master's direction. I was a young man of eighteen when
my master went to the mercy of God. I fell into an immense
affliction and great distress on this path, and God didn't open a
single door for me until the day that I had the vision, where two
drops or more fell on my heart from that intelligible universe,
after which it opened. I saw what I saw while I was travelling
in the universe of immersion for six or seven days, such that I
no longer perceived myself or anything else. The opening of
the door came to me as I was walking towards Kapulunca, for I
used to walk the route to the mountain twice each day.[32]

32. *Wāqi'āt*, fos. 34a–b. A story of Üftāde at his investiture as master, told to
his mother by a mysterious person, mentions that he should stay with her at that
time in Kapulunca and that he should do his retreats in the mosque at this place
(*Wāqi'āt*, fo. 40b).

The spiritual education of Üftāde

The master to whom Üftāde finally attached himself was called
Hızır Dede (d.913/1507).[33] Little is known about this person. Üftāde
must have met him at the age of ten while he was learning his trade.
He must then have begun to be initiated at a very early age by this
master, even though it was not the custom to train children so young.
It seems also that this affiliation could have been the real reason why
he felt repugnance for his job. Hızır Dede was a master belonging to
the Bayrāmiyye brotherhood, which takes its name from the famous
saint Haci Bayrām Velī (758–833/1357–1429), whose mausoleum is
to be found at Ankara.[34] There are several versions of his affiliation
to this brotherhood: he could have been initiated by one of the suc-
cessors of Haci Bayrām Velī, Akbıyık Meczūb (d.860/1456) or by
a son of Akbıyık or, again, by another successor of Haci Bayrām
Velī, Rüstem Halife. It seems, moreover, that he completed his spir-
itual education in the service of the successor of Hamdullah Çelebi,

33. Some sources mention that before him, Üftāde had been affiliated to the
Halvetiyye by the master Sünbül Sinān Effendi (d.936/1529). But this seems
highly unlikely because he would have had to have joined before the age of ten,
which was not the custom. Alternatively, he might have had contact with the
Shādhilī master Abdülmü'min (d.919/1513), and with Abdurrahman Efendi, who
was either Abdülmü'min's successor or, more likely, a master of the Kubrawī
order of Emīr Sultān (d.930/1524). See Bahadiroğlu, *Celvetiyye'nin piri Hz. Üftāde
ve dīvān'ı*, pp. 54–6; Öngören, *Osmanlılar'da Tasavvuf*, pp. 181ff.
34. He was the disciple of one of the most important saints of Bursa,
Hamīduddīn Aksarāyī, also called Somuncu Baba (d.815/1412), whose line goes back
to the founder of the Suhrawardiyya, Abū'l-Najīb al-Suhrawardī (d.563/1167).
He was also a close friend of the most celebrated saint of Bursa, Emīr Sultān.
His order, the Bayrāmiyya, occupies an important place in Ottoman Sufism,
particularly through its various branches. This order has, like the Nakşbandiyye,
the feature of a lineage going back to both ʿAlī and Abū Bakr. All that remains by
Haci Bayrām Velī himself are some poems and the *vird*, his master's daily litany
which he expanded. See Yılmaz, *Azīz Mahmūd Hüdāyī ve Celvetiyye tarikatı*,
pp.169ff. We may also note that he is very often mentioned by Üftāde in the
Wāqiʿāt.

Muhyi Efendi, who was also from a branch of the Bayrāmiyye.[35] All this allows us to affirm that Üftāde's master belonged to this brotherhood, all the more so since Üftāde indicates it himself in the *Wāqi'āt*, and there is no reason to doubt that he became a disciple of Haci Bayrām Velī.[36] This passage is particularly valuable, for in it Üftāde describes his early training with his master, and this allows us to dispel any doubt over his master's origins. Irène Beldiceanu-Steinherr has put forward the idea that Hızır Dede came from Moldavia and was from a Christian family. He would have been captured at the time of Fatih Sultan Mehmed's expedition in 881/1476 and brought to Anatolia. The idea that he could have been of Christian origin has been strongly contested by Mustafa Bahadiroğlu in his work on Üftāde. However, after reading what Üftāde says of him, one has to acknowledge that he certainly came from Moldavia and that he could have been of Christian origin, for we see him learning to do the prayers and the ablutions. On the other hand, one cannot maintain that he could have been captured so late and at the same time have been a disciple of Haci Bayrām Velī, because the dates do not correspond. Here is what Üftāde says:

> My master was a shepherd originally from Boğdān (in Moldavia). He came to live in a village in the district of Manisa. He was then ten years old. But his legs got frostbitten, and a woman looked after him for the love of God until he was better. Then he went to the town of Manisa, and a man who looked after the baths took him under his protection and made him look after the cash-box. Then he came to Bursa. One day, some time later, he came to the mosque of Kaygān, where he learnt from a man how to make the ablutions and pray. He helped at an assembly where the imam instructed him. He became one of the wayfarers. He dedicated himself to the spiritual life in this mosque during the day, and spirits came to him to teach him the Way. Then he put on the frock of the dervishes from the hands of

35. Kara, *Bursa'da Tekkeler ve tarikatlar,* pp. 101ff.
36. *Wāqi'āt,* fo. 74a.

Haci Bayrām. He then installed himself in a cell close to the court opposite the door of the Great Mosque, and he lived there until his death. He was one of those whose spiritual renunciation cannot be described and whose words cannot be understood. I was his disciple for eight years when I was a child, but the door was not opened for me during my master's lifetime. It was only later, after him, that the four degrees were opened for me, and the masters of our time are ignorant of these even if their actions are not empty of them.[37]

Another passage indicates that Üftāde's master experienced great nostalgia for his homeland:

He came from the country of Meneşte, and he often praised his homeland, saying that it was full of fruit. Most of his vines were tall and the best had many branches. You could pick at least a full load of grapes from a single foot of vine. I met him one day and he gave me some books, but I told him I couldn't read them. He said to me: "Take them and you will become a traditionalist and a commentator, and when you have got there, don't forget our country: it needs to drink, for its inhabitants are thirsty." We knew that he was expressing himself with truthful sincerity, but I could not go to this country because I wished to perform my pilgrimage. I told him that I was going off in this direction. He replied: "There is not enough time left, so be with the Beloved wherever He is to be found, for anywhere in His company is the garden of paradise. Some gnostics have said: If those who are mad with desire were to be in paradise without the Beauty, they would suffer torment, and if they were in hell in His company, they would savour it."[38]

37. Ibid. fos. 74a and 96b.
38. Ibid. fo. 78a.

His master Hızır Dede

Üftāde confirms that Hızır Dede was a farmer, which is why he
was nicknamed Çoban Şeyh. His account also shows that he must
have been Christian and then been converted to Islam, perhaps
even before coming to Bursa, when he had frostbite in his legs and a
woman cared for him "for the love of God", as Üftāde describes. He
looked after sheep and drove them to graze for the benefit of butchers
in the district of Mihaliç. He might have even been a butcher him-
self. He got frostbite in his legs while looking after the sheep, and
he remained paralysed before coming to Bursa. On the other hand,
his initiation into Sufism by Haci Bayrām remains doubtful, for the
dates do not exactly correspond, unless he lived until a very advanced
age.[39] Nevertheless, it seems that he was a mystic of the type called
uwaysī, like Üftāde, but in this case even before being affiliated to a
brotherhood. Another passage seems to indicate that Hızır Dede was
a disciple of Tāceddīn Ibrāhīm Karamānī (d.872/1467–68) and of
Şeyh Vefā (d.896/1491), who were, respectively, the second and third
successors in Bursa of the founder of the Zeyniyye.[40] Üftāde recounts
that: "one night Karamānī put on a frock in the place of a shirt at
the hands of Hızır Dede, who was in his service and in that of Şeyh
Vefā. He also recounted that he paid for his learning in the form of
a white bird at the time when he was living at Saint Sophia."[41] Hızır

39. According to Ismail Hakkı, Hızır Dede met Haci Bayrām when he came
to Bursa to make a pilgrimage to the tomb of Emīr Sultān. *Kitāb-ı silsile*, p. 76.
40. The Zeyniyye was founded by Zeynuddīn Ebū Bekir Hāfī (d.838/1434–
35), and spread throughout Anatolia. It resembles also the Suhrawardiyye and
the Rifā'iyye, and likewise goes back to both 'Alī and Abū Bakr. Öngören,
Osmanlılar'da Tasavvuf, p. 185ff.
41. *Wāqi'āt*, fo. 78a. In a passage where he recalls the forms which clothe the
spirit in visions (horse, bird, etc.), Üftāde mentions that some saints use the form
of a bird to travel in the world, as they cannot do so in their own human form,
that being a privilege reserved for the prophets and the most perfect saints (ibid.
fo. 97b).

Dede seems then to have also lived in Istanbul, and had already a bond through inspiration with his Zeyniyye master.

Hızır Dede had the reputation of having a profound knowledge of pharmacopoeia, and excelled in dream interpretation, as was to be the case for Üftāde. The latter recounts an episode where he was treated by his master:

> My master also possessed the spiritual power of breath. One day I caught dysentery and I had no medicine. I told my master who said to me: "Buy two dirhams' worth of different sorts of honey and mix them with bread, then you will get well." I did this and I didn't have another trace of dysentery. Another time I was suffering from a head cold, and I told my master. He took me to the water which ran in the Vā'iziyye, and said to me: "Uncover your head and put it under the water", which I did until he said it was enough, and I was cured.[42]

In another passage of the *Wāqi'āt* Üftāde speaks again of the dysentery episode, and recounts that after having been cured by his master he received permission from him to give treatment in the same way. However, he makes clear that the remedy does not reside in the nature of the medicine. "I found out that the cure was to be found in my master's breath and not in what I had eaten."[43] Hızır Dede did not mix willingly with people and lived a life of retreat. This is no doubt why he seems to have had no disciples other than Üftāde and perhaps a dervish called Mehmed Dede. His tomb is to be found in the Üçkuzular district above the cemetery of Pınarbaşı. Hızır Dede seems to have become a widower after coming to live with all his family in Bursa.[44] He used to spend almost all his time engaged in prayer and invocation at the Ulucami, where his disciple brought him food.

42. Ibid. fo. 37a.
43. Ibid. fo. 89b. See also fo. 96b for the blowing of the breath as a remedy.
44. The mention of his family means that he cannot have been single. *Menākıb*, p. 51.

Hızır Dede and the interpretation of dreams

Üftāde recounts also what his master said regarding the interpretation of dreams. For example:

> Whenever Hızır Dede interpreted a dream, he asked the one who had had the dream if he accepted his interpretation. When he replied "yes", Hızır Dede said: "Then two witnesses have confirmed it: one is my interpretation, and the other is the agreement of your reason. When something is confirmed by two witnesses, it is accepted both in the law and the spiritual way."[45]

As this passage shows, the interpretation of dreams in the spiritual quest is founded on a very strict principle for Hızır Dede. Üftāde explains it in the same passage, after having told his disciple that he must dedicate himself to the invocation of the formula of unity (*lā ilāha illā 'llāh*) until "the traditions of the Prophet and his path appear to you, in such a way that you no longer need to have recourse to any other source to be informed." He receives that by means of unveiling in dream, but he is not conscious of the meaning of that which he perceives, and must then follow his invocation until the knowledge is given. These unveilings need to be interpreted by the master. But for that it is necessary that they agree with the law, which is a condition imposed by Hızır Dede. Accordance with the law would remain a foundation of the mystical thought of Üftāde, who once, in traditional manner, criticised Hallāj for having missed this rule in his moment of drunkenness. "Unveiling can only be interpreted when reason remains perfectly in its place, so that one can hear the buzzing of bees, and if reason is disrupted, it cannot be interpreted. If the unveiling agrees with reason and this accords with the law, then it is accepted." Reason is here the necessary intermediary which provides the link between the law and the unveiling, between the exterior and

---

45. *Wāqi'āt*, fo. 66b.

the interior. It is in this respect that unveiling is really, for Üftāde, the foundation of spiritual experience, and provides the mystic with the basis for imitating the Prophet. While reason may be a criterion for the validity of visionary experience, unveiling is not to be interpreted by reason: "The true interpretation of dreams is only possible by the light of God."[46]

This light is given to the master who has traversed the four spiritual stages and has reached the summit of spiritual experience, which is the contemplation of God's beauty after annihilation. Then the interpretation of dreams is given to him for the purpose of spiritual direction. This light appears in the spiritual director, and manifests itself in the interpretation of dreams as inspiration. "One cannot interpret dreams by approximation, but only by inspiration coming from God."[47] The interpretation of dreams may also pose a great danger, if it is not performed by a perfect master. The exact interpretation "in right terms" is a superior stage, which is acquired by the unveiling of meanings. It is not the act of a single science alone. It results from being given a specific spiritual stage of perfection: the path of visible light. It is not sufficient, according to Üftāde, to travel through the places of manifestation of the most beautiful names by virtue of knowledge. It is necessary to "travel the path of visible light" in the unveiling, and then turn towards the places of manifestation, if one wants to pass beyond a station.[48] Thus the interpretation of dreams cannot be objective; it is tied to the spiritual rank of the one who interprets. It is in this sense that some of the perfect ones who have not reached this degree are unable to interpret dreams correctly and can cause serious harm to people by misleading them. Üftāde notes that it is the same for people of the exoteric. If exoteric knowledge cannot serve in dream interpretation, that is because it does not pass beyond the state of particular reason. In other words,

---

46. Ibid. fo. 52a.
47. Ibid. fo. 53b.
48. Ibid. fo. 78a. This point also refers to the vision that Üftāde had of the limits of the Halvetiyye, in which the mystic travels in the Names, whereas in the Celvetiyye it is the way of pure Unity.

the mystic who possesses the ability to interpret dreams is precisely one who has reached the universal intellect, whose visible form is the Archangel Gabriel, or the sacrosanct spirit present within oneself.[49] If there cannot be a science of dream interpretation, it is also because the same dream seen by several people will have a different interpretation according to the nature of each person, and will require its own unique treatment. Some interpretations of dreams return to a prophetic model, that of Joseph, but, Üftāde says, he cannot be imitated because of the nature of this exercise. The master states that he himself directed his heart towards the prophet Joseph in order to receive the inspiration of God but without imitating him. The fact that it is not objective prevents it from being taught or imitated, which explains why those who imagine they can employ formulae borrowed from their own master constantly make mistakes and mislead people.[50]

Visions and the law

Üftāde regarded the law as the essential criterion for the validity of vision. This is why reason is restored to a central position. It is the judge of the soul, he says elsewhere, and it allows one to truly find the meaning of unveiling by translating it into actions. From his master Üftāde maintained a very strong attachment to the law, as he expresses in the *Wāqi'āt*: "My master said: 'If all that is found in this lower realm and the angelic realm unveils itself to you and you find it in keeping with the law, then I consent to it; if not, leave this unveiling alone, but do not abandon the law.'"[51] When describing the Prophet's ascension, he says that first of all it involves ascending to closeness, and then returning to guide others on the spiritual path.

---

49. Ibid. fos. 78a and 91a.
50. Ibid. fo. 92a.
51. Ibid. fo. 30a.

In the same way, he insists on the fact that one can reach the purity of actions, where they conform to the prophetic ideal, only after having reached mystical knowledge. "To act in true conformity to the exterior sciences is only possible after having reached the knowledge of the four degrees (law, path, knowledge, reality)."[52] Certainly it is not actions which allow one to reach knowledge, for knowledge is acquired by the constant invocation of the formula of Unity and the name of God, *Huwa* (*Hū* = He), as he repeats untiringly in his poems. However, knowledge is not an end in itself: it is fulfilled in the reality of actions, for divine Unity must be known in the multiple and not in one's annihilation, even if annihilation of self is the ideal. In all these cases the law is, nonetheless, preferable to states and unveilings, and the Celveti mystic never ceases to seek out the most perfect expression. Furthermore, the most elevated unveiling for Üftāde is not that of the Throne or other marvels, but that of the soul's faults. This allows us, we should emphasise, to re-evaluate the classical works of Sufism, which analyse the soul's faults, and to link Üftāde's teachings back to the oldest methods in Sufism, such as the examination of conscience. But once again exterior knowledge is incapable of making one act in conformity to the prophetic ideal. It has a kind of "constitutional inability", as one can see in imposed forms of religion, for sincere action depends on the heart, and that can only engage in right action when it is purified by spiritual education, by practising invocation which allows one to reach the level of ardent love of God. "Some learned men asked me in Constantinople about the difference between exterior knowledge and interior knowledge. I replied: 'Exterior knowledge gives information about precepts, while interior knowledge guides you until you act according to these same precepts.' My reply amazed them."[53] Interior knowledge is the condition of fulfilling exterior knowledge. While the latter allows you to recognise and to judge, it can neither direct nor lead to realisation. On the contrary, it is completed through interior knowledge, which determines and precedes it, as Üftāde personally experienced.

52. Ibid. fo. 76a.
53. Ibid. fo. 76a.

The law occupies a dominant place in the way Üftāde conceives of spirituality. He recommends that his disciple follow the law in everything, but not by means of imitation, for that is worth nothing according to him. We find him praying to God to: "place us amongst those *on whose hearts faith has been inscribed* (Q.LVIII.22), free us by Your Gentleness from the quagmire of imitation, let us reach by Your Grace the reality of faith and the perfect affirmation of Unity, amen."[54] Asking God to liberate him from imitation does not constitute totally rejecting it, for it tallies with the aspiration to leave one stage in order to attain a new one. This is why, Üftāde explains,

> there are for us three stations: that of imitation, which is for the common run of people; the second is the stage of realisation and conviction *(īqān)*, and is for those who strive in interpretation, like the four imams; the third is that of contemplation and vision, which is for those who have arrived and the perfect amongst the people of the spiritual path.[55]

Imitation is not therefore a major obstacle. It is also a method but of a lower level, which requires to be gone beyond to the two higher methods. Imitation is even, as shown in another passage, a kind of connection, which links the prophets to the learned, and guarantees the spiritual cohesion of the hierarchy of religious functions in the community. Thus some of those learned in exterior knowledge "attach themselves to people of the Way and imitate them, for they are imitators of the prophets, who are realised and not imitators. But perfect saints are also realised ones, by virtue of their intercession." Imitation thus constitutes a genuine system of copying, in which the prophets represent the complete model, examples of reality which the lower levels can only reproduce. The saints are, for Üftāde, distinguished from the prophets in this scheme, and have a place in this

54. Ibid. fo. 12a.

55. Ibid. fo. 34b. Let us note in passing that this scale is not without ulterior motives, since Üftāde uses it to establish a three-part classification of the community: the community of believers, the learned, and finally the mystics whose special aptitude resides in vision.

social organisation only because they are actually intermediaries, the first rung of the ladder, who participate in the origin solely by virtue of the prophets' intercession and not by their own efforts.

On the other hand, he states that "the four stations (law, path, knowledge, reality) are like classes of vision: if one is defective, the others are good for nothing, and it is the same for the state in the stations. Now the law encompasses all the others, so that it is essential for the seeker to look after the law and maintain the custom of the Prophet."[56] Furthermore, the principle that not a single stage should be defective is a necessity which forms part of observing the law, so that the law conditions all of the four stages that one must traverse to reach spiritual perfection. He links this concern to the teaching of Ibn ʿArabī who, he recounts a little later, used to say: "I dedicated all my efforts to observing the custom of the Prophet, and I succeeded in following them all except one, and I was at fault because of that one." Üftāde also severely criticises those who do not grant Ibn ʿArabī the veneration that he deserves, maintaining that they fall into free-thinking and heresy. This point deserves to be noted, since it demonstrates that for Üftāde one of the most important lessons of the *shaykh al-akbar*'s teaching was conformity to the law, and the fact that finally everything comes down to fulfilling the law. As Michel Chodkiewicz says, "The spiritual quest is completed through that by which it was started: observance of the *sharīʿa* [law]".[57] Üftāde criticises Hallāj for having missed an essential principle of spiritual perfection by neglecting reason, and says that he stayed on the shore of the ocean of annihilation. For him observance of the law is intimately connected to the role of reason on the spiritual journey and in the acquisition of perfect sainthood. This requirement stems from the fact that for Üftāde the Celveti way is the way of the prophets, as he says several times. According to him, the behaviour of the prophets did not admit madness, but rested on the security of reason.

56. Ibid. fo. 88b.
57. M. Chodkiewicz, *An Ocean Without Shore*, Albany, NY, 1993, p. 116, and see all of Chapter 5, pp. 101ff.

This is why "the perfect one in the station of perfection is perfect through reason, to the point that he can hear the buzzing of bees at the moment he is drowned,"[58] which means that he is still master of his judgement at the moment he is nonetheless annihilated, that he is sober in his drunkenness. The persistence of reason is the perfection, for it is also the possibility of spiritual direction. The Quranic verse "He is the First and the Last, the Apparent and the Hidden" (Q.LVII.3) corresponds to the four stages which lead to the realisation of the verse "No divinity except Me, adore Me" (Q.XX.14), which is firstly the annihilation of one's own existence and the affirmation of the real Unity, then the stage of spiritual direction, which "weighs upon the shoulders of the one who reaches this stage".[59] The law, good works, are essential to sainthood, and "sainthood is not given to the saint before he reaches perfection in good works."[60] Observance of the law is a permanent requisite of sainthood, which can never be abandoned. In other words, sainthood will never have any connection to the eschatological expectation of abolishing the law, which would come down to abolishing creation, which is God's order. On the contrary, in one respect sainthood is the reaffirmation of the validity of this order. Consequently, "those who reach reality only arrive after having perfected their relentless determination to observe the station of responsibility that was laid upon them, without neglecting the least part, and we have never heard talk of a perfect saint who would have neglected something required by the law. Furthermore, the perfect saints, even after they have observed the legal obligations, customs of the Prophet and the supererogatory acts, observe only the least good practice of religion." So much so that "any saint who omitted only one good practice would not be perfect in sainthood."[61]

---

58. *Wāqi'āt*, fo. 88a. He also specifies elsewhere that the mad cannot reach perfection because they have lost their reason (ibid. fo. 94a).
59. Ibid. fo. 88a.
60. Ibid. fo. 24a.
61. Ibid. fo. 50a.

Spiritual direction

The spiritual director maintains the law and requires the interpretation of dreams to guide his disciples. Üftāde defines the qualifications of a spiritual director in these terms: "The spiritual director must possess three things: the knowledge of the learned, the wisdom of the wise, and the medicine of the doctor."[62] This definition may appear surprising. It refers to an ancient vision of the mystical master, who it is thought should master all the sciences of his time. The elements that Üftāde describes may seem exterior, but he gives them an interpretation which is clearly mystical. Thus "the perfect spiritual director possesses the knowledge of divine medicine, but the science is not that of [ordinary] doctors."[63] It involves a very different type of knowledge to the one suggested by the terms used. Spiritual direction can only be acquired with the three qualities mentioned. It is an intrinsic element of the Muhammadian perfection, for it is obtained at the end of a spiritual ascension and a re-descent towards the creatures; this follows the example of the Prophet's ascension, which took him to the highest station, closeness, before his re-descent for spiritual direction.[64] For Üftāde, the ascension provides the example for the Celveti spiritual way. The traveller should pay no attention to what he sees on the path to God, for "that becomes an obstacle to the truth" and, "if he becomes distracted on the way, he will not reach his goal," in the same way that the Prophet:

---

62. Ibid. fo. 14b. One must note that for Ibn ʿArabī the measure of wisdom is "the perfect combination of knowledge and practice", which is particular to the *malāmī*, the highest degree of accomplishment of perfect man. See W. Chittick, *The Sufi Path of Knowledge*, Albany, NY, p. 174. On wisdom in the early period of Sufism and its interpretation by Tirmidhī, see G. Gobillot, *Le Livre de la profondeur des choses*, Lille, 1996, pp. 49–55.

63. *Wāqiʿāt*, fo. 91a.

64. Ibid. fo. 15a. For the ascent and re-descent towards the creatures as the accomplishment of saintly perfection according to Ibn ʿArabī, see M. Chodkiewicz, *Seal of the Saints*, Cambridge, 1993, the whole of the last chapter.

did not turn towards the marvels of the world and the angelic realm on the night of the ascension until he had reached the station of closeness, and then returned to his place for the purposes of spiritual direction, and he contemplated the totality of things so completely that he could explain what is to be found in the gardens of paradise and the fire, in order to tell us about what he had been shown.[65]

This manner of contemplating the spiritual journey is of paramount importance for Üftāde. It is very similar to what has already been mentioned on the subject of knowledge, where Üftāde warned that it is necessary to travel in light in order only later to come back to the places of manifestation of the divine names. This arc of descent is essential to spiritual direction, since ascension demands the effacement of everything that is not God, so that there is nothing else but God. And ascent to God ends in annihilation: "when the affirmation of Unity reaches the secret consciousness, the traveller has only one single concern left, God the Most High, in such a way that all that which is other than Him is removed and there remains in him no place for spiritual direction."[66] Total annihilation (*al-fanā' al-kullī*) does not in itself enable one to direct others, but it is the station of spiritual directors, for it is the consummation of the spiritual quest. It is the ultimate point of "sainthood, which is apportioned to saints by the Pole of Poles", except for the "solitary ones" (*afrād*), "who have no need of the Pole".[67] Self-annihilation is

65. *Wāqi'āt*, fo. 15a.
66. Ibid. fo. 93b.
67. According to Üftāde, there are two Poles, one in the terrestrial realm and the other in the angelic realm, *Wāqi'āt*, fo. 3a. Üftāde mentions a story concerning Abū Yazīd al-Bistāmī, for whom he had so much admiration that he constantly cites him in the *Wāqi'āt*, and about whom he says he wrote a work: "when al-Bistāmī arrived at the station of proximity, a voice called out: 'By what way have you come to Us?' He replied: 'I have brought four things which are not in Your treasure.' Abū Yazīd said: 'When I pronounced these words, I was told: "Cross the threshold, for you have come guided by a venerable direction."' He went on: 'When I entered, I saw nothing in this station other than me, and so

one of the key points in Üftāde's spiritual conception, because, he says, "annihilation, worthlessness, humiliation and supplication are most loved by God, more than any other sort of action, for through humiliation the creatural condition appears, and through the appearance of the creatural condition one knows the lordly condition of one's lord."[68] In addition, it constitutes for him a crucial difference between the Celveti and the Halveti.[69] For the Halveti, spiritual direction is linked to a specific name that has guided the mystic in his ascension and his descent, and thus limits the capacities of this direction, whereas the Celveti, to the extent that they depend on the affirmation of Unity, can reach total annihilation and encompass all the places of manifestation.[70]

There exist many kinds of spiritual direction, each adapted to the individual. The spiritual director "has four chambers in accordance with the four stages, in each stage there is a room, and in that room his station is the highest, that is to say the reality. But he descends towards the nearest of the stages to guide the one who is searching. For example, he descends into the stage of corporeal nature, and he guides those who are found there by interpreting dreams and the thoughts which are dependent on them."[71] So every spiritual director possesses perfection in each stage, and can thus guide each person according to their level. Furthermore, this text suggests that one can have several different types of spiritual director according to the mission which is assigned to each. Some spiritual directors will be

---

I demanded His face, and was told: "This is not the station of anyone else; it is the station of the solitary ones (*afrād*), who have effaced their existence and are annihilated"'" (*Wāqi'āt*, fo. 15a). On the *afrād* and the Pole in Ibn 'Arabī, see Chodkiewicz, *Seal of the Saints*, pp. 53–4, 58, 107ff.

68. *Wāqi'āt*, fo. 15a.

69. The comparison between the two is a recurring theme with Üftāde and the Celveti masters like Ismail Hakkı, for the two ways have a certain relatedness, even if it is only because they have a common origin and their names only differ by a diacritical point.

70. *Wāqi'āt*, fo. 93b.

71. Ibid. fo. 78b.

more suited to guiding people belonging to this or that level, and the ways can be classified according to kinds of spiritual direction, the Celveti being, for Üftāde, the only way to reunite all the stages.

The task of muezzin

Üftāde accorded, as has been mentioned, a very prominent place to the interpretation of dreams in spiritual direction, and thus conformed to his master's principles. The *Wāqiʿāt* of ʿAzīz Mahmūd Hüdāyī recounts, on a day-to-day basis over some thousand pages, the young disciple's dreams and the interpretation that Üftāde gave to them. It is through this daily exercise of Üftāde systematically asking his disciple what he had dreamed, that the master could guide his disciple by giving his advice and evaluating the stage at which he had arrived. We may definitely conclude that this method was the one which Hızır Dede used, as described in the passage above. Üftāde had followed his teaching for eight years, from the age of ten, guided by a total love and infinite devotion for his master. He used to carry him on his back since he could not walk, to the great amusement of children who would shower them with jeers. On the other hand, an account in the *Menākıb* seems to place the meeting with Hızır Dede much later. This would mean that it was after Üftāde took up his post of muezzin that he started to study under his master's direction.[72]

> At the age of sixteen, wanting to perform the office of muezzin, he gave the call to prayer at the Great Mosque for a few brief years. One day one of the town notables died. One of the muezzins said to Üftāde: "So-and-so has died, so let us go and attend the funeral. We are bound to get a few pieces of gold." After the midday call to prayer, he agreed, saying: "Let us go and do it." Now by the side of the ablution fountain in the Great

72. *Menākıb*, pp. 106–7.

Mosque stood a spiritual master. He was called Hızır Dede, and he became Üftāde's master. He heard the exchange between Üftāde Efendi and the muezzin, and this late lamented master invited Üftāde to come to his side. He said: "Come and tell me, my child, what did you talk about with the muezzin?" He told him all about their conversation. When he had finished, he said: "Do not do what you said, my child. If you are in need, I will give you two pieces of gold every day", pulling two pieces from his pocket to give to him. He told him: "Come every day and receive two pieces of gold from me."

Üftāde and the sciences

In keeping with the way spiritual education was viewed in that period, Hızır Dede first of all wanted his disciple to train in exoteric sciences. The *Menākıb* describes how Hızır Dede made him begin by studying a well-known work of jurisprudence.

One day my master, the late Hızır Efendi, addressed himself to me saying: "Muhammad, we are going to get you to study. There is a work called the *Muqaddima* by Abū'l-Layth,[73] go and buy it." He gave me fourteen pieces of gold. As I was on my way to the market, having taken the money, there was a book-seller coming in my direction, with a book in his hand. I asked him what book it was. He replied: "The *Muqaddima* by Abū'l-Layth." I asked: "Are you selling it?" He replied: "Yes, I am." I asked: "How much does it cost?" He told me: "Fourteen pieces of gold." I took out the money, gave it to him and took the book to my master. I read it two or three times as a student with my master, after which all of the sciences were unveiled to me.[74]

73. *Al-Muqaddima fī'l-fiqh* is a work of jurisprudence often commented upon, written by the imām Nasr ibn Muhammad Abū'l-Layth al-Samarqandī (d.373/983–84).
74. *Menākıb*, pp. 18–19.

According to another version, the master made another dervish, Mehmed Dede, read the book. During the first few days, Üftāde could not understand a word, but then, with prayers and questions addressed to God, a little later "the door of effusion of mystical knowledge opened."[75]

The *Wāqi'āt* shows that Üftāde had a sound knowledge of traditional disciplines such as grammar, the traditions of the Prophet, jurisprudence and Quranic exegesis. He also knew Arabic and Persian very well. He says that he would have liked to learn music at the time when he was muezzin at the Great Mosque of Bursa, but he was unable to:

> One day as I was walking in the direction of Kapulunca, sad that I could not study, I met my master on the way. He said to me: "Don't be sad, for you will excel in this art." God then guided me in a manner which one cannot describe, and desire took hold of me. I left to make the call to prayer before dawn, and returned home only after the night prayer, and it was thus that when I started the call to prayer, people gathered under the minaret, profoundly moved by the sound of my call.[76]

However, he doesn't seem to have studied very long, and he probably would not have done so if he had not been pushed by his master. It is unlikely that Üftāde continued with his studies after his master's disappearance. According to Ismail Hakkı,

> while studying grammar, all the sciences were unveiled to him, in such a way that he no longer needed a teacher, and he began to pass on what he knew to those seeking knowledge, and he no longer needed to make the effort to study. It was such that whenever he intended to give sermons or advice he would have a vision of Mevlānā.[77]

75. Bahadiroğlu, *Celvetiyye'nin piri Hz. Üftāde ve dīvān'ı*, p. 42.
76. *Wāqi'āt*, fo. 14b.
77. Ismail Hakkı, *Kitāb-ı silsile*, p. 77.

Üftāde himself describes his being informed about the exterior sciences and the way in which he received direct training.

> At the beginning I dedicated myself to the study of general knowledge, until it was said to me that if I continued to study for twenty days I would be able to manipulate the world as I liked. So I stopped. By God, I did not accept, for mastering the world is worth nothing, and it was not thus that I would reach my aim. One can reach it only by self-annihilation, so I chose annihilation and I abandoned all else.[78]

He also learnt Persian through direct inspiration from Mevlānā Rūmī, as is reported in the *Menākıb*:

> One of the dervishes, Velī Dede, recounts: "One day I came to see the master to ask him to interpret a vision. Hearing some-one talking in the room, I remained waiting at the door. After a moment when the discussion had finished, the master invited me to come in, and asked me if I had been there a long time. I replied: 'Yes.' He continued: 'Did you not hear a discussion?' I replied: 'Yes.' He said: 'I had the honour of receiving the venerable spirit of the Pole of the gnostics, succour of those who have arrived, the author of the *Mathnawī*, Celāleddīn Rūmī. He brought me the noble *Mathnawī*. I said that I did not know any Persian. He told me to bring it at once.' The master ordered me to go immediately and buy a copy, as he had been told to do, and after that he quoted the *Mathnawī* many times in the gatherings."[79]

According to Ismail Hakkı, Üftāde had met Rūmī in dreams and the latter said: "'Transmit my book, the *Mathnawī*, in your sermons.' I said to him: 'But I do not know the Persian language at all.' He

---

78. *Wāqi'āt*, fo. 48a. Mastery of the world is also a particularly grave danger in Üftāde's eyes, for, as he says in a passage which recalls Ruzbehan Baqlī's warnings: "The last thing which emerges from the heart of the sincere ones is love of power" (ibid. fo. 7b).
79. *Menākıb* p. 27.

continued: 'Start to read and the language will be unveiled to you.'
In fact I went to sleep in Turkish and woke up in Persian."[80] The
Wāqi'āt shows that the master regularly turned to the *Mathnawī* in
his lessons and sermons. Üftāde also seems to confirm this kind of
training by inspiration in Persian through his initiatic bond with
Rūmī, in the *Wāqi'āt*. "One day I said to Mevlānā (Rūmī) that I did
not know the *Mathnawī*. He taught it to me, making me thus attain
knowledge of the seven degrees."[81]

If Üftāde was able to benefit from the spiritual influence of Ibn
'Arabī and mentions him quite regularly, he was perhaps even more
guided by Mevlānā, in particular by his great work in verse, the
Mathnawī, a book which is without any doubt the one most often
mentioned in the *Wāqi'āt* and from which the master drew a great
many teachings. This connection with Rūmī was so important that
Üftāde found it necessary to quote the *Mathnawī* systematically and
draw a large part of his teaching from it. This connection seems to
have been a very long-standing one, and began in his youth if we are
to believe the *Menākıb*:

"When I was young, a mystic from Bukhara arrived in Bursa,
and everyone in the town regarded him with reverence and
sought his prayers. One day after I had visited him, he presented
me with an enormous work. I said to him: 'My prince, I have not
reached the degree which would allow me to read this book. It
would be a waste.' He said to me: 'A day will come when it will
be necessary for you.' So I accepted it. Many years and months
later, when I thought of opening it in order to begin reading it,

80. Ismail Hakkı adds that in each sermon Üftāde used to quote several verses
of the *Mathnawī* and commented upon it "in the language of the Sufis" (*Kitāb-ı
silsile*, p. 77). See also Mehmed Şemseddīn's *Yādigār-ı şemsī*, p. 61.

81. Bahadiroğlu, *Celvetiyye'nin piri Hz. Üftāde ve dīvān'ı*, p. 43. The *Mathnawī*
seems to have remained an important reference for Celveti masters, some of
whom also had a privileged relationship with Rūmī, like Ismail Hakkı who is
said to have received in a dream the whole of the first volume of his commentary
on the *Mathnawī*, the night after his disciples' request that he write one. Ismail
Hakkı, *Rūh al-Mathnawī*, Istanbul, 1287, I, pp. 2–3.

I realised that it was the *Mathnawī*." Üftāde Efendi is said to have concluded each of his sermons and lessons by quoting a distich of the *Mathnawī*, and after pronouncing the final verse he said that there was no need to add a commentary.[82]

The way of acquiring knowledge through inspiration, which is shown in the case of Üftāde, as it is reported in the Celveti tradition, corresponds precisely to his theoretical position expressed in the *Wāqiʿāt*. With reference to his first training, he recounts:

> I went to learn the science of grammar from a man who lived at the Vāʾiziyye medrese. I had two lessons with him. On the third day he said to me: "O He who observes a teacher! In the end I only gave you one lesson, while you have already learnt two." Then these words poured forth from my tongue: "I confide my fate to God" (Q.XL.44), and I stood up to leave him. I did not return to anybody else. I prayed to God with humility and I wept in a mosque where I used to perform the call to prayer for the sake of God. Then the Book of illumination and all the other sciences were unveiled to me. Students gathered round me, and I gave them lessons with enthusiasm and kindliness, until some of them said : "We have had enough of the cheerfulness of your face." It was not long before that person who lived at the medrese fell ill and died. The pillar of all these quests is the affirmation of Unity.[83]

Later Üftāde describes how these sciences were revealed to him in the following words:

> Then he recalled the splitting of his chest, saying: "One day I saw that I had a chest in which there descended two drops or more of the intelligible world. My chest split open, and then all that was to be found in the universe was unveiled to me. It

82. *Menākıb*, p.126.
83. *Wāqiʿāt*, fo. 30b.

was as if it spread out before me, and thus I had the knowledge
of things which I had observed in the world and which corre-
sponded to them. Then other universes were unveiled to me,
one of which I saw was full of people, whose nearest dwelling
was vaster than those of the great ones of this world. Then I
saw another universe, in which the age of its inhabitants did
not go beyond forty, where the houses were made of stone and
people's clothes were taken straight from trees, because they
were not capable of making anything. After that I saw another
universe, whose inhabitants formed a single house larger than
our world. I questioned one of them who told me it was the
world of Babel." Then the master added: "The seeker should
pay no attention to his route, nor even to paradise, for it is an
obstacle to the Truth."[84]

We can see the role that inspiration plays in the acquisition of
knowledge for Üftāde. As he explains it, the essential factor for him
resides in the affirmation of Unity; this is, according to him, the dis-
tinctive feature of the Celveti discipline, which is thus distinguished
from the Halvetiyye, which is founded on the names of God. Üftāde
does not cease to remind his young disciple, ʿAzīz Mahmūd Hüdāyī,
to hold on to the affirmation of Unity, which does not negate other
practices, notably retreat and fasting, but which constitutes the basis
of all practices and of existence (itself). The sciences are given in
addition. They are not the essential, but they nonetheless form part
of the master's spiritual viaticum. He advises his disciple to look for
knowledge within himself:

He gave me some works of Quranic exegesis, and said to me:
"My son, these books are about this abundant science, but strive
until you can contemplate the meaning of God's words in your
own heart, and you can read it in your own thought, for science
is that knowledge there. At the moment you are unlettered,

84. Ibid. fos. 30b–31a.
85. Ibid. fo. 91a.

37

empty of the science that I have mentioned, so much so that you
know nothing, and he who has no knowledge can do nothing."

The knowledges with which Üftāde was favoured were then specific,
intimate sciences acquired in the heart through spiritual elevation.
The heart, Üftāde often repeats in the *Wāqiʿāt*, must become a blank
sheet, upon which sciences are written, such that the mystic can
read them within himself like a book. In effect, he says, "when the
seeker approaches real knowledge, all sciences leave his heart."[85] The
knowledge of which Üftāde is speaking is intelligible knowledge,
that which is symbolised by milk, the milk in the middle of which
his mother had seen him when he was still a baby. "Milk symbol-
ises knowledge, and knowledge does not refer to formal sciences,
for knowledge is actually intelligible, whereas exoteric sciences are
nothing but moulds and wrapping."[86]

In fact the science of common sense, that which is acquired by
study, can become a major obstacle to vision and knowledge in the
real sense. Üftāde recalls the case of some learned ones like Ghazālī
who, according to him, "spent twelve years struggling without ob-
taining the epiphany of attributes, for science is a hindrance which
becomes an obstacle to the truth."[87] He is even harsher towards Ibn
Sīnā (Avicenna), and he repeats an old tradition widely prevalent
amongst the Kubrawiyye, according to which "reason in the journey
cannot be independent, and because he wanted to use reason freely,
Ibn Sīnā was cast into hell."[88] In the same way he considers sciences
to have no value in themselves. He recounts a story about Ibn Sīnā
to illustrate the vanity of acquired science:

86. Ibid. fo. 83a.
87. Ibid. fo. 31a.
88. Ibid. fo. 51a. For the Kubrawī critique of Ibn Sīnā, see H. Corbin, *Avicenne
et le récit visionnaire*, Teheran, 1954, II, pp. 282–3. Simnānī gives another version
of it: "I asked: 'What do you say of Ibn Sīnā?' The Prophet replied: 'He is a man
who wished to reach God without passing through my intermediary, so I pushed
him back with the hand, thus, and he fell into the fire.'" The same judgement
against Suhrawardī al-Maqtūl follows. In addition, Simnānī has certain specific
criticisms of Ibn Sīnā – see Sijistānī, *Chihil majlis*, Teheran, 1366, p. 184.

One day a saint said to him: "You have spent all your life on rational sciences, what degree have you reached?" He replied: "I have found a particular moment in the moments of the days, where iron becomes soft." The saint said to him: "Show me the moment." When he found it, he showed him, he took a piece of iron and pierced it with his finger. After the moment had passed, the saint asked him if he in his turn could pierce it with his finger. He replied: "No, that belongs to the particularities of the moment and that has passed." The saint took the piece of iron and put his finger through it, and said: "A reasonable man must not dedicate his life to vain and ephemeral things."

And Üftāde recounts a similar story on the subject, regarding the learned Nāsir al-dīn Tūsī, who underwent a comparable misadventure on the subject of astronomy:

One day he went to the house of one of God's friends to visit him. Someone said: "Here comes the learned man of the universe, Nāsir al-dīn Tūsī." The saint asked what was his perfection. They said: "He has no equal in astronomy." The saint replied: "The white donkey is more knowledgeable than him." Tūsī was mortified. He left the gathering, and decided to go the same evening to the door of the mill-house. The miller said to him: "Go into the house, for there will be heavy rain tonight." Tūsī consulted the stars, but as he noticed nothing that would cause rain, he did not enter. When night fell, the rain was so strong that if he hadn't taken refuge on the doorstep, he would have been carried away by the torrent. He asked the miller how he had known. He replied: "When a white donkey makes his tail move in the direction of the sky three times, it means it will not rain, but if it is towards the ground, rain will fall." When Tūsī heard that, he recognised his own helplessness.[89]

89. *Wāqi'āt*, fo. 51a. According to Üftāde, astronomy was transmitted by David, but it has become corrupted, for David possessed it by prophetic revelation and only used it to guide men towards faith (ibid. fo. 27a).

Interior direction

Üftāde was particularly affected at the age of eighteen by his master's death. He had only been with him for eight years. Furthermore, at the death of Hızır Dede, he had not yet reached the level of perfection required, as he himself explains:

> When I was eighteen, my master rejoined the other world. I remained prey to terrible grief and immense suffering. In this state God did not open a single door to me. One day I saw some drops fall from the universe of meanings onto my body. After that it opened. All that I could see I saw after that. Then I fell into the universe of drowning, and I journeyed there for six or seven days. There remained for me neither soul nor anything else.[90]

This passage shows that Üftāde followed his spiritual journey without a living master. This is why the older writers such as Ismail Hakkı considered him to be a mystic of the *uwaysī* type, that is to say initiated by a hidden master. He also seems to have been guided by the greatest master (*al-shaykh al-akbar*), Ibn ʿArabī, as is explained by Huseyn Vassāf following Ismail Hakkı: "Üftāde drank from the same source as the *shaykh al-akbar*, pride of those who come after, and epitome of teachers. After the death of his spiritual director, Hızır Dede, he received the influx of the spiritual realities of the *shaykh al-akbar*, as one can read in the *Wāqiʿāt*."[91]

Üftāde shows great veneration for Ibn ʿArabī in the *Wāqiʿāt*. He bears witness in a striking way to the position occupied by the teaching

90. Kara, *Bursa'da Tarikatlar ve tekkeler*, II, p. 106.
91. Ismail Hakkı, *Kitāb-ı silsile*, pp. 78–9; Mehmed Şemseddīn's *Yādigār-ı şemsī*, p. 62; Vassāf, *Sefīne-i Evliyā*, II, pp. 621–2. Ismail Hakkı declares that he also had an initiatic contact with Ibn ʿArabī, who gave him three pieces of advice during a vision: to avoid coloured clothing in order to reflect Unity; not to lean on a stick so as to rest only on God; and to avoid contact with people (*Sharh al-usūl al-ʿashara*, Istanbul, 1256, p. 28).

and person of Ibn ʿArabī in the conception of mysticism in the following passage: "After the companions, those who have reached the rank of the *shaykh al-akbar* are very few. Those who are incapable of perceiving his rank fall into heresy – may God protect us – but those who realise the Unity, who have reached the four degrees, inherit from him the divine impeccability."[92] In the same way he says: "After the companions, there was nobody like him apart from five or six people."[93] In another passage further on, however, he states:

> I have been a companion of Ibn ʿArabī in my contemplations. I asked God one day what was the rank of Abū Yazīd al-Bistāmī, and He told me: "He is an accepted servant close to Me, I love him and I love whoever he loves." Then I set down in writing his virtues so that by his love I might be loved by God. Now I found in the account of his virtues that he had said: "One day I saw all the dead men, and I pronounced four times the formula 'God is Great.'" The *shaykh al-akbar* had said: "This is what the master Abū Yazīd has stated, but he should have said: 'I saw myself dead, and I pronounced the formula "God is Great" for myself.' For what is appropriate for the perfect one is to limit one's regard to examining the faults of one's soul and not to go beyond this limit and into the faults of others." I then said to the *shaykh al-akbar*: "In this matter you yourself examined Abū Yazīd's condition in a critical fashion," and when he heard me he was silent.[94]

This passage shows that while Üftāde had a great veneration for Ibn ʿArabī, he equally felt an immense veneration for Abū Yazīd al-Bistāmī who is, along with Rūmī, by far the most-often mentioned mystic in the *Wāqiʿāt*. Üftāde had also been initiated by Ibn ʿArabī in the manner of *uwaysī* Sufis, and he was, like all Ottoman mystics, a supporter of the Unity of Existence, *wahdat al-wujūd*, the formula

92. *Wāqiʿāt*, fo. 29a.
93. Ibid. fo. 32a.
94. Ibid. fo. 8b.

which sums up the subtle doctrine of Ibn 'Arabī, even if he himself only mentions it once, in his weekly litany (*Wird*). He confirms the inspired character of the *Futūhāt al-Makkiyya*, the great work of Ibn 'Arabī, saying: "When the greatest master composed the *Futūhāt*, he contemplated spiritual meanings and set down what he had contemplated, without involving the lesser talent of a writer."[95]

Üftāde the preacher

He must have begun the job of muezzin at the age of sixteen, and continued for eighteen years at the Great Mosque. He also, at about the same time, took up the post of imam and gave lessons in various mosques.[96] From the age of thirty-four he seems to have taught his disciples in mosques, places that he particularly loved, after the manner of his master, since he preferred them at first to a dervish lodge. He preached every Thursday at the Dohan Bey mosque using it like a lodge, and on Fridays in different mosques where people crowded in to listen to him. The *Menākıb* describes his sermons:

> Kastamonī Şaban Dede recounts: "When I was in Kastamonū, I had a vision in which I saw a moon rise from Bursa and I heard a voice say: 'Rejoin your master!' After I woke up, I told my parents that my brother would remain to serve them as I was going on a journey. They would not let me, but since I was adamant, they eventually changed their mind. I arrived at Iznik at the lodge of Eşrefzāde, who told me to wait and see what was to be. The same night I had a vision in which I heard: 'Rejoin your

---

95. Ibid. fo. 8b. This statement corresponds to what Ibn 'Arabī himself says in the *Futūhāt al-Makkiyya*. See amongst others, Chodkiewicz, *Seal of the Saints*, p. 18. For Ibn 'Arabī's *Wird*, see the reprint of the Ottoman edition, Oxford, 1979; we can now use P. Beneito and S. Hirtenstein's translation, with excellent introduction, entitled *The Seven Days of the Heart* by Ibn 'Arabī, Oxford, 2000.

96. *Menākıb*, pp. 47, 81–2.

master in Bursa.' In the morning I left for Bursa with my master's permission. I arrived on a Thursday, and Üftāde Efendi was preaching in the mosque of the late Dogan Bey. I saw that there were so many people that many had their feet jammed up against the skirting. I sat down at the end of the platform. I squeezed myself in. When the gathering was over, everyone got up to kiss his hand. When I myself came close to kiss his hand, the master said to me: 'At last you have come.' I replied: 'Yes, my prince.'"

Subsequently, he preached again in the mosque of Kayagan, and it is there that his disciple, the prolific author of mystic works, 'Azīz Mahmūd Hüdāyī, met him and bound himself to his service.[97] In that period he displayed great energy having mosques built or small places of worship enlarged into great mosques, where he spent his time preaching.[98] Somewhere between the ages of forty and forty-eight he was appointed as official preacher at the Emīr Sultān mosque, a position he held right up to the end of his life. This followed a vision in which "Emīr Sultān spoke to Üftāde, saying: 'Are you not going to come and see me? It is time, come!' Üftāde replied: 'The order belongs to you: if you command it, we will come', getting up to make his way to the Abode of felicity."[99] According to Ismail Hakkı, he had first of all refused this responsibility, when people pressed him to accept. Then, after a vision in which Emīr Sultān said to him: "Agree to serve and preach in our mosque", he had finally consented, but without taking for himself the salary which would have come to him. He divided the four pieces of money that were due to him daily amongst the dervishes who made their retreat in the mosque.[100] In addition, Üftāde confirms having seen Emīr Sultān "twice in his mausoleum, the body still fresh, of medium height, dark skin, with

97. Vassāf, *Sefīne-i Evliyā*, II, p. 631.
98. *Menākıb*, pp. 54–5, 86.
99. Ibid. p. 71.
100. Ismail Hakkı, *Kitāb-ı silsile*, p. 79; Vassāf, *Sefīne-i Evliyā*, II, p. 623.

a small beard like yours".[101] Muslihüddīn Efendi, who had made a strong impression on Üftāde in his youth, would have intervened on his behalf so that he would accept the teaching post at the Emīr Sultān mosque, as the master recounts in the *Wāqiʿāt*:

> As for the post of teacher at the mosque of Seyyid Buharī (Emīr Sultān), I did not accept it because it was a position in the public eye, but Seyyid Buharī asked me himself. Then he spoke to one of the men gifted with unveiling, named Muslihüddīn, saying to him: "If he has some regard for me, why will he not agree to preach?" One day after that, when I had not yet clarified the ins and outs of the job, the nomination arrived from the sublime porte, which said that the secretary's son was ill and asked if I could write something for him. I wrote it and when it arrived, God cured him. That was a visible sign of the good of the sender of the nomination. For one who attains your rank, neither public office nor high rank could do him any harm.[102]

The nomination had become a subject of discussion at the highest level of State because the mausoleum of Emīr Sultān occupied a symbolically important position, as this personage had been Bayezid I's son-in-law and spiritual master. One day when someone recalled the memory of Emīr Sultān in the Imperial Council in the presence of ministers and the highest religious authorities, they went on to discuss the Kükreh-Zāde, who was preaching in the mosque attached to his mausoleum. "The preacher there is an enemy of spiritual masters. He is unfit to fulfil this function." On being asked who could take up this office, one of the ministers mentioned Üftāde's name. Unsure whether he would accept, they decided to write down his nomination immediately and to send it as quickly as possible. Üftāde then accepted, and prepared himself to go and preach the following Friday. His predecessor, who had been ousted, meanwhile decided to take revenge by hiding under the pulpit formulae taken

101. *Wāqiʿāt*, fo. 39a.
102. Ibid. fo. 38a.

from the Quran for the purposes of sorcery. Üftāde came to know of this through unveiling, and sent in advance a carpenter, telling him to saw the feet off the pulpit chair, so that it would be lower. The carpenter found what was hidden, and took it to the master, who despite all that did not bear any grudge against this person.[103]

It was at the same time that he settled on the mountain above the cemetery of Pınarbaşı, founding a dervish lodge attached to a little mosque, which still exists, in which to direct his disciples. There he continued to preach the precepts of the law, whilst putting his disciples through forty-day retreats, through which they found purification and opening of the heart. The lodge did not accept offerings of meat that came from sacrifices. It was also shut to women and children, and a severe discipline must have reigned, for the master imposed an almost total cutting-off from the world in the lodge.[104] At the time of the commemoration of the martyrdom of Husayn, the Prophet's grandson who was killed at Karbala, he had *aşūre* made, the traditional dish for this occasion. For the Night of Destiny, during Ramadan, all the supererogatory practices required were accomplished, and for the anniversary of the Prophet's birth the master made them recite the *mevlid*, the praise of the Prophet.

Üftāde died on 12 Cemāziye'l-evvel 988 / 26 July 1580, in Bursa. He is buried by the side of a mosque, where his mausoleum is still much frequented. Today Üftāde's lodge still dominates the town of Bursa, the old Ottoman capital, built high up against the mountain. One can still see there the hall where the dervishes used to gather for sessions of group invocation, the front-room where he received visitors, and the room to which he withdrew to devote himself to his invocations and litanies, sitting in a small niche carved out of the wall, where he would pass the night, his legs tied together, so that he could not fall asleep when he became drowsy during the long spiritual night exercises.

103. *Menākıb*, pp. 71–2.
104. Ismail Hakkı makes clear in one of his works that Hüdāyī was only allowed to go and visit his family once a week (*Sharh al-usūl al-'ashara*, Istanbul, 1256, p. 28).

The principles of the Celvetiyye according to Üftāde

Üftāde is the founder of the Celvetiyye brotherhood. The Celvet-
iyye is usually considered one of the branches of the Bayrāmiyye,
as has already been mentioned.[105] In fact the spiritual line of Üftāde
goes back through his master Hızır Dede to Haci Bayrām Velī. The
lineage is established as follows:

Üftāde	d.988/1580
Hızır Dede	d.913/1507
Akbıyık Meczūb	d.860/1455
Haci Bayrām Velī	d.833/1429
Hamīdüddīn Aksarayi	d.815/1412
'Alā'uddīn 'Alī Ardabīlī	d.833/1429
Sadruddīn Ardabīlī	d.794/1392
Safiyuddīn Ardabīlī	d.735/1334
Ibrāhīm Zāhid Gīlānī	d.700/1300
Jamāluddīn Tabrīzī Azhari	d.672/1273
Şihābuddin Tabrīzī	d.638/1240
Qutbuddīn Abharī	d.623/1226
Abū'l-Nacīb al-Suhrawardī	d.563/1167
'Umar al-Bakrī	d.487/1094
Kādī Vahyuddīn	d.452/1060
Muhammad al-Bakrī	d.400/1009
Muhammad Dīnawarī	d.367/977

105. Üftāde acknowledges in the way of Haci Bayrām Velī the merit of
invoking the formula of Unity, and states that they use four of the names that the
Halvetiyye employ. He makes a distinction, all the same, between the Celvetiyye
and the Bayrāmiyye by saying that his way uses three further names, and that
it includes the interpretation of conscious thoughts and dreams (*Wāqi'āt*, fo.
102b).

Mumshād Dīnawarī	d.299/912
Junayd Baghdādī	d.297/909
Sarī Saqatī	d.253/867
Maʿrūf Karkhī	d.200/815
Dāwud Ṭāʾī	d.184/800–01
Ḥabīb ʿAjamī	d.150/767
Hasan Basrī	d.110/728
ʿAlī ibn Abī Ṭālib	d.48/668
Muhammad	

One of the points of debate regarding the Celvetiyye is the problem of knowing who really founded this brotherhood. As we have seen, it is difficult to say with certainty from whom Hızır Dede received his investiture. The fact remains that he belonged to the Bayrāmiyye. This brotherhood comes from the same source as the Safaviyye, which later gave rise to the Safavid dynasty in Iran. The mention of Üftāde's spiritual lineage is to underline the ties by which his lineage is joined to other lineages. The most important link in this respect is Ibrāhīm Zāhid Gīlānī. His role is important for several reasons. Firstly, Ismail Hakkı makes him the founder of the Celvetiyye, because he is the first to have introduced the invocation of twelve names, the seven names of annihilation plus the five of subsistence.[106] Others trace the foundation of the Celvetiyye back to Haci Bayrām Velī, because he gave a major role to the invocation of the formula of Unity, *"lā ilāha 'illā llāh"*. These statements only demonstrate in the end the characteristic concern of Sufism to guarantee the practices of the brotherhood by illustrious predecessors supposedly giving their blessing to a new brotherhood. The fact that Üftāde had inherited older practices reveals nothing beyond the fact that he is the founder of a specific brotherhood, and that it is his own spiritual impetus which gave rise to the emergence of a brotherhood with

---

106. *Kitāb-ı silsile*, p. 108. However, he affirms at the same time that the true founder of the Celvetiyye is Üftāde.

enough character to last until the twentieth century. Furthermore, and this is one of the most interesting elements in the mention of Ibrāhīm Zāhid Gīlānī, Üftāde several times is at pains to carefully distinguish his brotherhood from his own path of the Halvetiyye. For Ibrāhīm Zāhid Gīlānī is the link to whom both the Celvetiyye and Halvetiyye trace themselves back.[107]

Again, we must bear in mind what Üftāde tells us himself about his spiritual education, when he states that he did not reach unveiling until after his master's death and was guided interiorly by Ibn ʿArabī, Rūmī and also, according to a passing remark by ʿAzīz Mahmūd Hüdāyī, Emīr Sultān, who asked him in a vision to preach at his mosque, a duty that he carried out until the end of his life, which would be about fifty years later. This direct teaching is also a fundamental element of the Celvetiyye, and confers on it a particular identity. Furthermore, it is difficult to maintain that Üftāde was his master's official successor, since at his death he had not yet reached the level required for spiritual direction, which as we have seen requires that one has gone through the four stages of the spiritual path as defined in the Celvetiyye. Üftāde passed these four stages through his interior initiation with the masters mentioned above. In addition, he once explains more explicitly to his disciple what happened to him on the way to Kapulunca, when he reached that stage of reality. "Then there was the unveiling of the master of light-filled Medina, the gift of reaching annihilation, which he accorded me, and the gift of spiritual succession (*khilāfa*)."[108] This passage confirms that Üftāde received his investiture directly from the Prophet, and explains why he constantly returns to the idea that the Celvetiyye way is that of the Prophet and his companions. Thus the Celvetiyye possesses specific characteristics, not the least of which is to be the inheritor of a direct teaching through unveiling by Ibn ʿArabī. It is that which leads Mustafa Bahadiroğlu, with good reason, to assert the original

107. For Ibrāhīm Gīlānī, see Yilmaz, *Azīz Mahmūd Hüdāyī ve Celvetiyye tarikatı*, pp. 154ff. For a discussion of the attribution of the Celvetiyye's foundation to Üftāde, see Bahadiroğlu, *Celvetiyye'nin piri Hz. Üftāde ve dīvān'ı*, pp. 189–98.
108. *Wāqiʿāt*, fo. 109a.

character of the Celvetiyye, and re-open the whole question of the affiliation to the Bayrāmiyye, which rests on well-attested historical foundations, but which, from a spiritual point of view, neglects the interior nature of Üftāde's initiation, and overlooks the specificity of his teaching.

The specific character of the Celvetiyye stems also from the fact that Üftāde uses this name to designate his own path. He also recognises that it has specific methods which distinguish it from the other major ways of Bursa at that time, especially the Halvetiyye, for which the comparison is by far the most developed. For Üftāde the Celvetiyye is the way of the Prophet, which is a fundamental point in his eyes and repeated untiringly. He does not miss any opportunity to underline this distinctiveness. It is particularly the case when he deals with the problem of certain methods of the brotherhoods, like dream interpretation and conscious thoughts, which took on such importance in his eyes, as we have already seen. He also recalls that the Prophet used to interpret dreams like conscious thoughts. This allows him to distinguish three ways and to maintain the absolute fidelity of the Celvetiyye to Muhammad's teaching. According to him, in the way of Shaykh Maghribī, a Kubrawī master, one only interprets conscious thoughts and declines to do so for dreams, which are considered to have no value. In the way of Emīr Sultān, one refuses to interpret either of them, and only practises the prayers which are also, he says, highly effective. In the way of Haci Bayrām Velī, "one raises visionary perception through practice, practises the invocation of the formula of Unity", and employs four of the names of the Halvetiyye.[109]

---

109. "Conscious thoughts agitate the heart and make it flutter, like the wind agitates plants in the desert. The invocation of the formula of Unity in a loud voice makes them cease, and if one continues the invocation without their ceasing, then the seeker should complain about it to his master." Üftāde also makes clear that the method of spiritual exercises is very limited, for as soon as someone neglects them, they lose their rank. He adds: "Our way is that of the Prophet: we eat what we need so as not to become feeble in our worship, and we do not insist on spiritual exercises" (*Wāqiʿāt*, fos. 102b–103a).

Introduction

Celvetiyye and Halvetiyye

The comparison between the two spiritual ways, Halvetiyye and Celvetiyye, is very important in Üftāde's eyes. It is through this contrast that he is led on several occasions to clarify the specificity of his way, and as a result, to provide for it foundations, which enable us without any doubt to maintain that he really is the founder of the Celvetiyye. The comparison between the two rests first of all on their very great proximity. They both return to a common link in their spiritual line. Furthermore, their names are written in the same way in Arabic, except for the first letter of their names, which is marked by a diacritical point above the letter for the Halvetiyye and below for the Celvetiyye. This twofold resemblance justifies in itself the comparison between the two ways. However, the diacritical point which distinguishes them makes all the difference between the two, and Üftāde has fully explored this question, followed later by Ismail Hakkı.

The two ways bear names which refer to different types of spiritual experience and practice: *halvet* (or *khalwa* in Arabic) for the Halvetiyye, and *celvet* (*jalwa*) for the Celvetiyye. The two have their source in the example of the Prophet, who is first of all isolated by going into retreat (*halvet*) in the cave of Hira, cutting himself off from the world and men, in order later to direct people by mixing with them, lighting the way for them through his own enlightenment (*celvet*). Ismail Hakkı explains this difference by saying that there exist no other ways but these two. *Halvet* (retreat) corresponds for him to annihilation, as in the first part of the formula of the Muslim faith (there is no divinity other than God) and *celvet* (illumination) to the subsistence, as in the second part (Muhammad is the messenger of God).[110] Again, for him, the Halveti way is the condition of the Celveti way, for one can reach subsistence only by annihilation, and when one has reached that, one does not return

110. *Kitāb-ı silsile*, pp. 64–5.

50

to the other since subsistence goes beyond annihilation. In the first way the mystic no longer sees himself, while in the second he is re-installed in the contemplation of divine beauty and maintained in the face of it, which is why he can direct the creatures. Also, spiritual direction necessitates the return, the descent into creation. In this regard Üftāde criticises the Halveti way for designating someone as successor to the master, without taking account of whether or not he has completed his spiritual education by realising the four stages, which is inconceivable for the Celvetiyye – for them, only someone who has passed beyond the stages can be invested as a master, and this for him removes the risk of heresy.[111]

He also makes clear that the Halvetiyye is founded on traversing the names, the seventh stage depending on a particular name both in the ascent and in the descent, which means that spiritual direction is itself the function of this name and thus turns out to be limited. In contrast, the Celveti way is founded entirely on the affirmation of Unity; this is the "way of the prophets and the companions", which allows one to comprehend all the names.[112] Resorting to the affirmation of Unity as the practice of invocation appears to Üftāde to be a distinctive feature of the Celveti way, which thus attempts to link up with the manner of the Prophet and his companions. He states that this formula is incomparably more effective than the repetition of any other name whatever; even more, "it re-unites all the names". In a comparison between the two ways he suggests the inadequacy of the Halvetiyye, saying: "the people of the Halvetiyye arrive through the names and those of the Celvetiyye by the formula of Unity, but the path that the Prophet and most of his companions travelled was the Celveti way, and there is no success in any of the ways except by purification of the soul."[113] This constitutes a particularly strong critique of the Halveti way, since this purification is only possible by the formula of Unity, which it does not use in the same sense. Even further, he states that the formula of Unity encompasses all

111. *Wāqi'āt*, fo. 112a.
112. Ibid. fo. 93b.
113. Ibid. fo. 11a.

the names which the Halvetiyye employ, thus placing it above the other. The Halvetiyye rely on the invocation of seven names which correspond to the seven stages, according to Üftāde, as has already been indicated. On the other hand, the master sometimes tends to minimise the difference between the two ways. Thus in one passage he says that the two ways include seven stages, but the number of seven stages is obtained by adding to the four stages the three inter-worlds (*barzakh*) which separate them.[114]

The difference between the two ways is demonstrated particu-larly well, according to the master, in the attitude that they adopt towards unveiling. "We sometimes see the adepts of the Halvetiyye state that they have unveiling, and when we hear them, we think they have attained the reality (that is to say, the fourth stage), but it is nothing. As for the Celvetis, what they see is the recompense of their state."[115] The difference here rests as much on the attitude as on the nature of the unveiling. Üftāde finds fault with the Hal-vetis for displaying their unveiling, whereas he maintains, following Ibn 'Arabī, that the highest rank is that of the *malāmī*, the people of blame who hide their states. Furthermore, their unveilings are provisional and artificial, for they are not based upon an interior condition acquired by purification of the soul. On the other hand, the unveilings of the Celvetis are the graces that flow from the ac-quired station, which refers equally, in Üftāde's mind, to the idea that the station is superior to the state, and that spiritual experience reaches a stage where unveiling acquires a sort of permanence. It is the moment of the theophany of the essence which is the supreme accomplishment of the spiritual journey in total annihilation. For the Celveti way is the quest for total annihilation, which is also the station of joining (*cem'*). By annihilation the mystic completes the

114. Ibid. fo. 4b. The seven names of annihilation include the formula of Unity, and they are *lā ilāha illā 'llāh, Allāh, Huwa, Haqq, Hayy, Qayyūm, Qahhār.* By adding the five names of supra-existence (*Samad, Ahad, Wāhid, Fattāh, Wahhāb*), we get twelve names. On these names and the invocation in the Celvetiyye according to Hüdāyī, see Yilmaz, *Azīz Mahmūd Hüdāyī ve Celvetiyye tarikatı*, pp. 18ff.

115. Ibid. fo. 48b.

nature of his existence, for "all existents are perishing with regard to His existence, and if the existence of this universe were not a veil, all would be consumed by God's light. Even our existence is a veil which prevents union, and it is why those who have attained have devoted their efforts to annihilating their existence."[116] Annihilation thus completes the nature of existence, by doing away with the latter so as to allow only the divine light, which overpowers the mystic and achieves in him the Unity of existence throughout his aiming.

This is also why the journey has no end for the Celvetiyye, and can never lead to the suspension of the law or of the torment which affects the mystic in his spiritual quest. The Halvetiyye employ the forty-day retreat as a technique of spiritual perfecting, an exercise which has to be gone beyond. In contrast, for the Celvetiyye, the retreat and other types of spiritual exercises have no end. From this point of view, spiritual effort is not the same as a technique. It is a veritable way of life, through which the Celveti mystic follows unendingly the way of the prophets and the perfect saints, for the law, as we have already emphasised, is not suspended by perfection. On the contrary, it is an integral part of this perfection, which is attained by completely fulfilling the law and good practices. Üftāde recalls, on this subject, the discourse that he had with one of the successors of Sofyalı Bālī Efendi (d.960/1553), a Halveti master who came to see him:

> I spoke to him about the Halvetiyye, saying the journey through each of these seven states lasts no less than seven years. He replied: "They travel a lot in the imaginal world, but our Celveti companions travel so much in the specification (*taʿayyun*) that their journeying never ends." I went on: "You could well live to a hundred, and your journey would never end, since just as the

116. Ibid. fo. 45a. Üftāde's mistrust of unveiling was deep, as the following passage about miracles and spiritual powers shows: "The opening of one of the doors of affirming God's Unity is worth more than any sort of unveiling or spiritual power. But after perfection it is allowable for spiritual powers to appear, except that the authentic reality is total annihilation and drowning in the ocean of the affirmation of Unity" (ibid. fo. 57a).

One whose Unity is affirmed has no end, so the way of the one who professes His Unity has no end."[117]

This is why for Üftāde, the Celvetiyye is the way of the "people of torment", as Najm al-dīn Kubrā also said regarding his own path, in the prologue to the Quranic commentary which is attributed to him.[118] Üftāde also justifies this position through the nature of the reunion with God: "The flavour of the reunion is commensurate with the depth of the torment one undergoes on the way of the Beloved."[119] This torment is for him inseparable from the experience of unveiling, an experience which he nevertheless warns us to be cautious about. In contrast, the Halvetiyye rely on the taste gained in travelling through the names, and the experience of theophanic acts and divine attributes, as has already been mentioned. This way remains, for Üftāde, confined to taste, and lacks that which is the basis of all spirituality, the difficulties and calamities of the way.

This is also why the Halveti way can only reach annihilation at the end of its whole path, and does not attain it perfectly, whereas the Celvetiyye realise "total annihilation" at each stage of the journey, in order to really destroy the whole existence of the traveller. Thus,

117. Ibid. fo. 96b.

118. N. Kubrā/N. Rāzī, *'Ayn al-hayāt*, introduction. This conjunction with certain Kubrawī teachings is certainly no accident. Sometimes Üftāde quotes from memory passages from Kubrā's treatises, such as *Usūl al-'ashara* (*Wāqi'āt*, fo. 62b); or again, an unedited treatise on the Way, which compares mystical knowledge to the ocean and the Way to a boat (ibid. fo. 52a). It also seems that Muslihüddīn had a special connection to the Kubrawī saint of Bursa, Emīr Sultān, and we must not forget that Üftāde spent half of his life serving at Emir Sultan's mosque. Furthermore, we sometimes find in the *Wāqi'āt* mention of the following correspondence between the spiritual organs and visions of coloured lights: corporeal nature = black = earth, soul = red = air, spirit = yellow = fire, secret consciousness = white = water (Bahadiroğlu, *Celvetiyye'nin piri Hz. Üftāde ve dīvān'ı*, p. 212). We must also mention that in a letter to Ibrāhīm Efendi Hüdāyī recommends that he carefully read *Mirsād al-'ibād*, the great manual of Sufism by Najm-i Rāzī, one of Najm al-dīn Kubrā's successors (*Menākıb*, pp. 161, 165).

119. *Wāqi'āt*, fo. 103a.

in addition, the Halveti way aims at paradise, for it limits itself to journeying through the places of manifestation of divinity and to this contemplation. Concerning the four stages of the way, those of corporeal nature, soul, spirit and secret consciousness, the Halveti way can only reach, with difficulty, the third stage, in other words the first degree of the angelic realm which is also the stage of the elite – for the two first stages correspond to the terrestrial realm and the last two to the angelic realm. The Halvetiyye then can reach annihilation in theophanic acts and then the attributes, but cannot reach annihilation in the essence. This latter is precisely the experience of the Celvetiyye, which is only possible by the way of affirming Unity – accomplished by total annihilation and reserved for the privileged (elite) of the elite. Only the way of Üftāde allows one to reach true contemplation, or even substantial union, which is the degree of union. Total annihilation is accessible only in "the angelic realm and belongs to the Celvetiyye, whereas the sixth stage certainly exists for the Halvetiyye", that is to say, the stage of spirit, but only through mystical knowledge and not by spiritual state.[120]

For Üftāde, one of the great differences between the two ways stems from the fact that the Celvetiyye is the way of the formula of Unity, *lā ilāha illā 'llāh*, whereas the Halvetiyye is based on the invocation of the names. From this point of view, as has been mentioned, the Halvetiyye path cannot lead to perfection. In fact, it goes directly to the places of manifestation of the names before going through annihilation, so that it can never arrive at the true illumination by the names, which necessitates first of all the total annihilation of the traveller. It inverts the relation between annihilation and subsistence, between *celvet* and *halvet*, and thus in a certain way misses both of them. However, the Celveti way does not neglect the invocation of the names. In one passage, where Üftāde advises his disciple to emphasise the first part of the formula of Unity, that of negation (no god) to expel conscious thoughts, he goes on to recommend him to strengthen himself by invoking the name *al-Qawī* (the Strong).[121]

120. Ibid. fo. 63a.

In this comparison we cannot, however, confine ourselves solely to the ritual forms of the brotherhoods. We should also look at the relation between the two ways in terms of the reality of retreat and of enlightenment, inasmuch as they are spiritual experiences, the two being, as Ismail Hakkı said, the only two ways possible. Reflecting on the difference between the two can clarify the nature of the Celvetiyye. The emphasis laid on subsistence as the consummation of annihilation leads us to maintain a principle that Ismail Hakkı was able to employ on occasion, in order to justify certain very specific points of Muslim cultural practice. Üftāde finds fault with retreat for completely cutting out the unity of all creatures, and for losing at the same time the relation which intimately links divine Unity to the will of the Creator, since reality depends on Unity. There would be no creation without the irreducible multiplicity of beings, this infinite diversity whose secret lies in Unity, and which as a result only Unity can truly know. Consequently, to pretend to isolate unity in itself is to miss the meaning of what one thinks one is maintaining. Unity can only really be known in the vision of the multiplicity of creation. The superiority of the Celvetiyye over the Halvetiyye stems from this essential principle in Üftāde's eyes, and is the consummation of his way. Thus the Halvetiyye go astray, in one respect because of their desire to perceive the names and find subsistence without going through annihilation, and in another respect by their inability to go beyond isolation with regard to creation and be able to perceive the Unity in the multiple.

121. Ibid. fo. 29a. We may note that when his disciple asks him how many times he should repeat it, Üftāde tells him that in his way there is no specific number of invocations, and that he should repeat it until he feels its effect in him.
122. Ibid. fo. 42a.

The four stages

One of the elements upon which the doctrine of Üftāde rests is the idea that the spiritual journey consists of passing through four stages, which correspond to the subtle centres or spiritual organs. These are: corporeal nature (*tabī'a*), soul (*nafs*), spirit (*rūh*), and secret consciousness (*sirr*). "These four stages are the way of the prophets. The first two are a gift granted to the common run of people. The third is reserved for the elite, and the fourth for the privileged ones (elite) of the elite."[122] The carefully distinguishing of these four stages is essential in Üftāde's eyes. One should not mix them up, for the confusion which may come out of this mixing is a source of going astray and heresy.[123] One of the most remarkable aspects of this scale is that the heart is not part of it, and that it ignores the degree of complexity which people at that period had come to in analysing these subtle centres.[124] The aim of the mystical journey is union with reality. But, says Üftāde, this is a result, like the fruit is the produce of the tree, and consequently depends on it. The order of the stages is comparable to a tree and its roots.

> It is necessary to reach perfection in the law so that the road opens towards the way, and this towards mystical knowledge and then the reality. Each subtle centre has to be built up by that which corresponds to it. Thus to corporeal nature corresponds the law, to the soul the way, to the spirit the mystical knowledge, and to the secret consciousness the reality.

When all these structures have been built in their appropriate place, which is reminiscent of platonic doctrine, "all that is left is union (*wusla*)", which in some way results from the equilibrium of the whole but is not solely in the traveller's power.

123. Ibid. fo. 25b.
124. On spiritual organs in Sufism, see G. Gobillot and P. Ballanfat, "Le coeur et la vie spirituelle chez les mystiques musulmans", in *Connaissance des religions*, Jan–Sept 1999 (57, 58, 59).

One day, Hüdāyī asked him a particularly pertinent question about the completion of the spiritual quest, following a talk by Üftāde: "The master said: 'The traveller does not reach his goal without abandoning the world here below and then the body, the spirit and finally the secret consciousness.' I then asked: 'If he abandons all that, then with what does he arrive?'" The question is crucial. It springs inevitably from the idea of self-annihilation. If one annihilates oneself, how can one still have a spiritual experience, and if one maintains oneself, how can there be reunion between God and His creature? Üftāde's reply beautifully clarifies his ideas about fulfilling the spiritual quest. He explains that, on arriving at total annihilation, the traveller is as if recomposed by order of God and participates, in a certain manner, in His existence, in a tone which recalls Najm al-dīn Kubrā's insights in his Quranic commentary:

> He replied: "Then comes God's impulse, which is the intention behind His word: 'We offered the trust to the heavens, to the earth, and to the mountains; they refused to undertake it and were afraid thereof; but man undertook it (Q. XXXIII. 72).' When this impulse arrives, the body stays in one place, the soul in one place, the spirit in one place, and the secret consciousness in one place, that is to say each is situated in a [different] stage. It is not that they are reduced to nothing, for nothing has here the meaning of being put in order. The traveller acquires the reality of intelligible existence, which is proper to union."[125]

The traversing of the stages results, then, in putting the subtle centres in order, each in the place due to it, and this interior restructuring spiritualises the body/existence, in which the mystic is as if transfigured. That is only possible, Üftāde clearly stresses, by divine intervention and does not depend on the traveller's particular merits. It involves a sort of supreme gift by which the mystic is raised up, placed beyond his immediate existence, provided with a new form, which includes a body that alone allows one to reach union,

125. *Wāqiʿāt*, fo. 103a.

for it is adapted to the divine existence, according to the principle dear to Najm al-dīn Kubrā that the self is known only by the self. This intelligible existence is an eternal body , which arises from total annihilation and is the condition for reaching God: "The reaching to God the Most High is only possible by abandoning on the way the body and the spirit, and by annihilating existence. If the traveller annihilates his ephemeral existence in this ephemeral world, he will reach eternal existence in the eternal world."[126]

This is how Üftāde deals with the question of the relationship between the mystic who reaches his aim and the divinity. He wishes to show how union is realised while maintaining the duality between the mystic and God.

> When he has annihilated his existence, he is reduced to nothing, and that which is nothing is subject to nothing thanks to unification and to incarnation. In fact when we speak of unification, we mean drawing close, which is accomplished through conformity to the satisfaction of God, like when one says that so-and-so is united to so-and-so, insofar as it leaves no doubt that it involves two independent people, in reality and in meaning. He is reduced to nothing insofar as he vanishes and disappears in the ocean of drowning and the lights of theophany, if we consider that all that is other than God has disappeared from his eyes, so much so that he looks and no longer sees himself, because his orientation towards God has been fulfilled.

Thus, once again, he is not reduced to nothing, his "otherness" is not removed. It is properly put aside, suspended by the fact that he is turned totally towards God, forgetting himself. His annihilation is not substantial, merely intentional. In God's eyes, he is maintained as a different person, which is why unification or incarnation can never denote a substantial fusion, but only the annihilation of self for the self. "When one has annihilated the existence of the secret consciousness, and there remains not a single trace of it, one is

126. Ibid. fo. 10a.

given another existence, which is raised up by the theophany of the essence."[127]

This particular feature of the completion of the spiritual journey is, in Üftāde's eyes, an immense secret which he says he wanted to hide but it slipped out. Thus he actually explains the nature of spiritual realisation, which consists in the link that ties the essence to the witness, difficult to describe other than as being elevated to another level of existence. This level cannot be described as other than the effacement of the secret consciousness, the strange forgetting of self by the self. "It is like someone who looks at the sky, and no longer sees the sky, or who has risen so far that he no longer sees the one lying down."[128] The purification of the heart has no other meaning than to guarantee the integrity of the aspiration. Annihilation, then, denotes nothing other than the unflinching direction of the gaze, which implies that the subject is absorbed not in the object but in vision. Emerging from himself, he is the gaze suspended by the grace of God, he is nothing but pure relation. There cannot be any question of fusion. On the contrary, the essential otherness of God is realised by the mystic's leap in his aspiration. Eternal existence, the intelligible body, is no other than this equilibrium of aspiration maintained between the two, where duality is abolished without otherness being lost, something which Rūzbehān Shīrāzī summed up particularly well by comparing the aspirant (*murīd*) to an arrow which flies without ever hitting the target.[129]

---

127. Ibid. fo. 104b.
128. Ibid. fo. 98b.
129. Rūzbehān, *L'ennuagement du coeur*, Paris, 1998, introduction, p. 69.

Annihilation and knowledge

Total annihilation allows one to arrive at knowledge of the essence. Üftāde classifies knowledge into sciences of possible existence and sciences of necessary existence. The first are not true sciences, for they also include nothingness. On the other hand, the second exclude nothingness, for their object is necessary existence. Amongst these, there is firstly the knowledge of the lordly condition, which the mystic arrives at only after having known his own soul, according to a well-known saying attributed to the Prophet: "He who knows his soul knows his lord." Beyond this knowledge is another knowledge, that of divinity, but while the first is built on maintaining the subject who knows himself, this second one necessitates total annihilation and absolute effacement, for it is knowledge of the essence which surpasses knowledge of the attribute.[130] Such total annihilation, which the master also calls the station of joining (*cem'*), consists of seeing none other than God, and it goes beyond the station of coincidence (*ma'iyya*) in which one sees at the same time God and creatures.[131] Thus this other existence, this separation of self from self, is again a form of knowledge, knowledge of the manifestation of the essence. Man thus realises his humanity, which consists of three degrees: human, angelic and superior. The superior level is characterised by a knowledge whose nature and way fall outside the known categories. The human plane corresponds, according to Üftāde, to the traditions of the Prophet (*hadīth*) and the angelic level to the prophetic revelation. There is a third level situated beyond and about which nothing can be said, except that it definitely corresponds to this knowledge of the essence, or again to pure theophany, for as Üftāde says: "Gabriel guided the Prophet by the intermediary of

130. *Wāqi'āt*, fo. 105b.

131. Ibid. fo. 62b. On the coincidence with the Essence, see my introduction to Rūzbehān, *L'itinéraire des esprits*, Paris, 2000, pp. 14–27.

revelation, and then he went beyond the Gabrielian nature under his direction."[132]

This is why for Üftāde the Celveti way is the way of annihilation, for it brings about the elevation of man beyond himself. This way is for him precisely what Shams-i Tabriz taught to Mevlānā, and which initiated the *Mathnawī*, the immense poem that served as guide for Üftāde all his life. "Mevlānā had not reached the stage of mystical knowledge, when Shams arrived. He guided him to knowledge, he made him ascend to a superior stage and showed him the way of annihilation." Men who follow this way are "people of annihilation, men of the hidden world who confine their affairs to God, who have annihilated existence from themselves by total submission and have attained total annihilation." This statement defines the ideal Celveti. Now these men, Üftāde says, have the feature of not being cut off from other men, although "their state is covered by a veil, and hidden from the knowledge of people, to the point that even their fathers, sons and wives cannot comprehend their states, even though they live with them day and night."[133] This remark allows us to understand the depth of Ibn 'Arabī's influence on Üftāde, for these men of the hidden world correspond precisely to the people of blame, the *malāmī*, whom the greatest master considered as mystics of the highest rank. Total annihilation, for Üftāde, is the mark of these men of the hidden world. It is "the authentic reality", "the drowning in the ocean of affirmation of Unity", which presents itself in visions as "drowning in a white ocean". In his eyes this annihilation is the most important. It is preferable to all unveiling and other spiritual powers, for these are merely favours granted in addition to the spiritual station.[134]

132. *Wāqi'āt*, fo. 55b.
133. Ibid. fo. 48a.
134. Ibid. fos. 57a, 59b.

The subtle centres

The subtle centres depend upon one another. They are like mirrors the one for the other, for the qualities and faults of each are reflected in the subtle centre immediately next to it. This phenomenon is most particularly evident in visions: "What we perceive in the vision of beautiful or ugly forms comes from the soul's reality, and the spirit takes form with those attributes. Even if the spirit is in itself subtle and pure, it takes the form provided by the soul's qualities because of the latter's reflection in it." It is the same for all the relationships be-tween the subtle centres, which reflect their beauties and impurities, the one in the other.[135] Thus each can purify the dross of the others: the soul the impurities of the corporeal nature, the spirit those of the soul and the secret consciousness those of the spirit. However, seeing the soul's impurities is not a failing, for

> the unveiling of one of the soul's faults is better for us than that
> of the heavens and of the earth; in fact its faults, its impiety,
> its straying are particularly well hidden, so much so that when
> they are revealed the seeker may turn it to good account, for he
> can be free of them, remove the obstacle which obstructs his
> path and reach his goal.

Üftāde's decided preference for this type of unveiling to that which might appear higher stems from the fact that for him self-know-ledge, that is to say knowing one's own soul, is the precondition to knowledge of the lord in his lordly condition. This is not to say that he rejects the unveiling of the realities of the world, like the heavens and the earth. But it is not of great use, and in addition, according to him, this unveiling is only given when one reaches the third degree, after having purified one's soul. When one has passed beyond this stage, two types of vision are given: "At the level of the spirit is the

135. It is worth adding some correspondences: to the four degrees correspond the four primordial elements and the four rivers of paradise (ibid. fo. 105a).

pure unveiling; then at the level of the secret consciousness is anni-hilation and theophany."[136]

The purification of the subtle centres

The four subtle centres have to be purified by the affirmation of Unity, so as to make them into citadels or fortresses which will pro-tect the mystic from that which is other than God. Each of these stages is a citadel or fortress in the interior of another: reality is a fortress within knowledge, knowledge within the way and the way within the law, the whole forming a citadel of four fortifications. The stages are thus wrapped one inside the other, and the master com-pares this phenomenon to clothes worn on top of one another.[137] The goal is at the centre of this system and acts on the mystic throughout his journey in each stage. The traveller goes through all these stages in one direction by annihilation, and then returns by subsistence. The two directions of his journey, ascending and descending, are important. In the ascent he forgets all that he passes through, for he progresses by annihilation. These fortifications are actually present, but without him being conscious of them, for in annihilation all intermediaries are removed. On the return he passes through the same stages, which are this time reaffirmed and become visible. This double movement of going by annihilation and returning by subsist-ence is required for him to possess spiritual direction, according to Üftāde who says: "All these stages are present in us. We see them and we go through them."[138]

One cannot reach the angelic realm of the last two stages without realising the first two. For "when corporeal nature is put to rights by the law, and the soul by the way, then the road is open towards the angelic realm, and so long as they have not been put in order, there

136. Ibid. fo. 32b.
137. Ibid. fo. 108b.
138. Ibid. fo. 50b.

is no path to the angelic realm." Üftāde compares the relationship of the four stages to a tree, referring to a saying that he attributes to the Prophet: "The law is the tree, the way its branches and knowledge its leaves." Commenting on this, he shows the interdependence of these four stages: "In the same way that the fruit issues only from the principle of the tree, thus it is with the law, and just as the tree without branches is good for nothing and produces no fruit, thus too is the way [...] It is the same for the reality, if the seeker reaches his origin."[139] The stages overlap each other in a way which makes the highest imply the return to the lowest, which is why it can be said that "the beginning of corporeal nature is its journey towards God and its end its journey away from God."[140] The law is the essential condition for reaching reality. It is like the other face for it, and communicates directly with it. In this relationship, the way and knowledge are merely the means, the link which unites the two principal elements, the most exterior aspect and the most interior, for the consummation of the mystical quest is not simple annihilation. Annihilation is the condition for returning to the entirety of the law, which has been finally realised, since, as has already been mentioned, the law can only really be completely fulfilled by one who has passed beyond all four stages to the point of total annihilation, in which the mystic gives himself up to the divine light.

This is why in this process vices are transformed into virtues by the realisation of the four stages. This phenomenon would have no meaning if the accomplishment of the spiritual quest ended only in pure annihilation. In fact the annihilation of which Üftāde speaks is not a suppression of the mystic's being, but a transfiguration in which he becomes pure aim, clothed in another existence but not abolished. The four stages correspond to the subtle centres of man's interior, which constitute the ladder of his being. Üftāde sums up in a short passage the internal composition of man and the nature of the subtle centres:

139. Ibid. fo. 57a.
140. Ibid. fo. 112b.

In man there are to be found four things: corporeal nature (or even, his humanity), soul, spirit and secret consciousness. Corporeal nature is composed of primordial elements: it has a base side which inclines towards illicit things, such as adultery, sodomy, consumption of alcohol and impure nourishment, for example, and an elevated side which urges one to avoid those things and to endeavour to render worship to God. The soul is a force which possesses seven attributes: pride, vanity, ostentation, jealousy, anger, love of good things and love of glory. It also has a base side and an elevated side: if one does not exchange its attributes of rebellion for attributes worthy of praise, it remains on the base side. But if one purifies it and transforms these attributes into virtues, it is pacified and finds itself addressed by the words: "[O peaceful soul] Come back to your Lord satisfied and satisfying" (Q. LXXXIX.28). It ascends then from the lowest to the highest. Their being put to rights is only possible through the mystical journey and serving people of spiritual direction.[141]

These two centres belong to the terrestrial realm. When the mystic passes beyond them, he reaches the angelic realm. The purification of the subtle centres permits them to acquire specific qualities, which are their condition and power of movement:

> In the purification of corporeal nature one acquires affection; in that of the soul one acquires love (*mahabba*); in that of the spirit one obtains fervent love (*'ishq*); and in that of the secret consciousness one obtains a state that the masters call "the valley of bewilderment", which consists in the traveller knowing his Lord and not being able to reach the point where his existence is annihilated, as long as union does not precede it.[142]

141. Ibid. fo. 107a.
142. Ibid. fo. 2a. On this idea, see also fo. 116a; and the same classification in fo. 112b, where the valley of wonderment is replaced by effacement.

This process is also the progress of annihilation, which takes each subtle centre to the height of its power. The qualities that are acquired in each subtle centre are a force which sets them in motion, in order to project themselves beyond themselves to the level immediately above them. This interior force is the ascending process of the heart. At each stage, the power of this subtle centre is converted into a higher power, more spiritual, until it reaches the threshold, where there is no other power than the supplication addressed to God, with full confidence in Divine Providence, as is so eloquently attested to in Üftāde's poems. The suffering to which he constantly refers is none other than Adam's affliction, by which he was taken back to his origin, and the visible signs of which are, as with Rūzbehān Baqlī, tears. Üftāde describes this process of annihilation and mutation in the following terms with regard to the first stage:

> When corporeal nature is restored, the power of affection which is found in the heart of the seeker ceases to turn towards all that which is not God, such that all of him gathers together and turns as one towards the love of God. Then, having reached the way he arrives at the soul. When that is put in order, the same takes place for the way and its vices are transformed into virtues, which allows him to go beyond the soul. Then he arrives at the spirit, and when the knowledge of God is realised, he goes beyond it and comes to the secret consciousness and from there unto God.[143]

Üftāde also makes clear in this connection that this process can give rise to the visualisation of lights, recalling the description of the light ascending from the heart to rejoin that which descends from God according to Najm al-dīn Kubrā, for at each stage the purification of the subtle centre causes a light to spring forth which rises as

---

143. Ibid. fo. 118b. The same passage indicates that this driving power inside the heart is the impulse from God and is nothing other finally than the divine trust for which man is responsible, as the Quran says (XXXIII.72): "We offered the trust to the heavens, to the earth and to the mountains, who refused to take it and were afraid, but Man took it upon himself, for he was unjust and ignorant."

far as the subtle centre above and so on unto God. This progress of annihilation is then at the same time the inward growth of the interior light of the heart, which ascends to rejoin its beloved and reaches the ultimate threshold in itself which is the secret consciousness, "that which is of the most noble in the man, for it is by it that he distinguishes himself from all the animals and reaches the highest treasures, which can only be reached by the heart."

The subtle centres and the scriptures

For Üftāde the people of annihilation do not look for unveiling and spiritual powers, for they follow but one unique goal, the affirmation of Unity through their total annihilation. To seek unveiling would completely contradict the very nature of their journey, which is a progressive effacement. This is one of the points which for him marks the difference from the Halveti way, as he says: "We have no spiritual unveiling or power other than to have certainty and faith, like the Prophet and the companions had faith."[144] Nevertheless, unveilings and other spiritual experiences are actually given to each level of the subtle centres in the course of the mystic quest. "When corporeal nature reaches perfection and truly becomes a corporeal humanised nature, the secret of the lordly condition reveals itself",[145] because perfection for the corporeal nature consists of total submission to the law. Thus it realises in itself the perfect condition of servitude, which implies at the same time the revelation of the divine sovereignty, for the servant is necessarily in the service of his lord. It is the same for the three other subtle centres. The purification of the soul gives rise to "the theophany of divinity" or again "the unveiling of the secret of divinity". At the level of the spirit it is "the unveiling of intimate knowledge" or "the secret of life and death", and for

144. *Wāqiʿāt*, fo. 113b.
145. Ibid. fo. 110b.

68

the secret consciousness "the theophany of reality in perfection by the perfecting of these stages", or again "the reality of the divine order".[146]

The doctrine of the four stages has its source in the division of the subtle centres. It is only later that it combines with the doctrine of spiritual stages. The reason for this relation for Üftāde is to be found in the nature of the revealed texts. At the same time, there is on his part a constant concern to found his teaching upon prophetic example, since the Celveti way is deemed to be the way of the prophets. This point also reflects the crucial importance of the texts and their nature. According to Üftāde, the two sources of authority for the Muslim, the Quran and the sayings of the Prophet, are divided into elements which reflect, respectively, the four stages. What makes the theoretical link between the subtle centres and their spiritual states can be found in the revealed texts, so that without these texts this relation would not exist, and the spiritual journey would not be possible. Thus,

> that which in the texts is linked to the corporeal nature is named law, that which is linked to the soul is named way, that which is linked to the spirit is named knowledge, and that which is linked to the secret consciousness is named reality. The whole is one with regard to divine wisdoms, and multiple with regard to the relations.[147]

The distribution of the foundational texts gives rise to an explanation of prophetic revelation. This was received by the heart of Muhammad, but the nature of what was revealed depends on the level of the subtle centres in which this revelation is shown.

> What was revealed to him at the level of secret consciousness is called Quran, and arrived in words and meanings; what arrived at the level of the spirit is called sacred sayings (*hadīth qudsī*) and only appears as meaning, for the words are the Prophet's;

146. Ibid. fos. 110b, 108b.
147. Ibid. fos. 97a, 29a–b.

69

what comes about at the level of human nature at the time of guidance is called prophetic sayings.[148]

These three levels of the word correspond also to three universes: that of reality, spirit and body. Addressing his disciple, Üftāde tells him: "You must pass beyond the world of bodies, then that of spirits, so as to arrive at the universe of reality."[149] This journey is also the route of the internal ladder of one's being, the itinerary of the subtle centres that one must simultaneously pass beyond and construct, and the crossing of the texts. In this way the mystic returns the most exterior speech, whose word and meaning belong to the Prophet, to its interior archetype, in which first of all the meaning is recovered in the universe of spirits, then the original words to which these meanings correspond. Thus we can understand better what accounts for Üftāde's idea that arriving at reality is at the same time returning to the origin. In fact it is a matter not so much of arriving at meanings as their textuality, that moment where the exterior is the most interior, where law is reality.

The subtle centres and the prophets

This supreme stage, where the interior and exterior are one and the same, is also the stage of the state of being beloved (*maḥbūbiyya*), which is reached when "the traveller goes beyond the stage of fervent love [...], except that one cannot reach the summit of the Prophet's state of being beloved, and were one atom of it to be granted to the worlds, it would be sufficient for them".[150] This stage is the highest, and is to be found above the stages of confidence (*khalīliyya*), which corresponds to Abraham, and of intimate converse (*kalīmiyya*), which

148. Ibid. fo. 97a.
149. Ibid. fo. 105b.
150. Ibid. fo. 59b.

is that of Moses. To the spiritual hermeneutic by which the mystic returns the body to its prototype, where words are their meanings, corresponds the ladder of the prophets of one's being, to recall Henry Corbin's handy expression, which comes from the Kubrawī master 'Alā' al-Dawla al-Simnānī. The journey of the stages is also a hermeneutic of the Quranic text, as Üftāde explains in a passage where he shows that the seven stages of the Halveti way are summed up in the four Celveti stages, to which one adds the intervals which separate them and which are the inter-worlds.[151] Going back to a saying that he attributes to the Prophet, "The Quran has an interior meaning and an exterior aspect, and that up to seven meanings", Üftāde explains that the journey of the four stages is also the pursuit of these seven levels of meaning, which are in the end nothing other than the seven mountains of our being which the Quran mentions, and which Najm-i Rāzī also takes up in his typology of the subtle centres. The four stages appear as a summary that includes multiple levels. They become more complex as seven levels, when we consider the discipline of the spiritual ways. But if we take into account the details of the mystic's journey within his own being, they form a total of 18,000 worlds, thrones, or specifications of essence (*ta'ayyun*) as understood when following the system adopted by the master. To travel the universe of our interior prophets consists in travelling the 18,000 interior worlds of man, which are the stages of annihilation.[152] In each of these universes or specifications of essence is to be found a prophet whom the mystic meets, and whose universe he must pass beyond, which he can only do through the intercession of Muhammad. If the Prophet's intercession is indispensable to the traversing of each universe, that is because he is the only one to have been sent after all the specifications and stages of prophecy have been completed. His status as seal of the prophets conferred on him the privilege of being

151. Ibid. fo. 4b.
152. These 18,000 stations of annihilation are summarised in a succession of spiritual experiences, beyond which there is no further qualification possible. They are faith, contemplation, vision, closeness, union and effacement (ibid. fo. 109b).

able to ascend and descend all of these stages and to fulfil the whole of the prophetic heritage. It is also why proximity to Muhammad is the highest degree of sainthood, even if the saints are differentiated according to the prophets to whom they are spiritually attached by what they have achieved.[153] These 18,000 thrones are in the existence of man, and the highest is "the place where God is manifested and where His knowledge is established". One can only reach the reality of this throne by the purification of the heart.

The journey of the thrones or specifications of essence ends in the major resurrection, which corresponds to the disappearance of the specification of essence itself. The mystic must arrive at the vision of this greater resurrection, which in the end is none other than the total annihilation in which all the realities other than God, that is to say the specifications of essence which can be seen, are effaced.[154] This station is "the station empty of specifications". The specifications of essence are the object of vision by a power of mind which corresponds to them. They occur through the mediation of Gabriel, although he can only be perceived as he really is by the Prophet, in the same way that divine wisdoms are acquired through the mediation of the Prophet. It is, however, possible to perceive the station of Gabriel, who is present in the atoms of all the specifications of essence, when one has passed beyond them all and reaches the station empty of specification, a station in which it is impossible to exhaust the entire number of steps, since the realisation of the affirmation of Unity is infinite.[155] For Üftāde, the one who has passed through all these stages and who has reached this station is the perfect man, an expression that he hardly ever uses. Üftāde once described the vision that he had of this perfect man, who in his appearance brought together the four stages: "During one of my retreats I saw a man who had four faces on the four sides of his head, forming a perfect whole

153. Ibid. fo. 18b.

154. "The death of the individual is the lesser resurrection, and the death of the specifications of essence is the greater resurrection" (ibid. fo. 112b).

155. Ibid. fo. 108b.

of great beauty. This manifestation appeared ten years after God had opened up the four stages for me, and the faces were the sign of these stages."[156]

The caliphs and the subtle centres

In the same way that the spiritual journey unfolds like a hermeneutic and as a journey of the prophets of our being, so the four stages have a relation to the first four caliphs who succeeded the Prophet. Here again historical reality is tied, for Üftāde, to the doctrine of the four stages but does not directly follow the chronology of the caliphate. He mentions that the pulpit where Muhammad preached was made of four steps. For Üftāde the number naturally corresponds to the four stages. He says, moreover, that Abū Bakr, the Prophet's first successor, preached from the third step, which corresponds to mystical knowledge. These indications allow him to establish a correspondence between the caliphs and the stages of the mystical journey. Thus ʿUmar, the second caliph, embodied the law, because he refused to accept the Prophet's death due to his love for his person. ʿUthmān, the third caliph, represents the way; Abū Bakr, the first caliph, mystical knowledge; and ʿAlī, the fourth caliph, reality.[157] Naturally the master makes clear that each of the four had fully realised the four stages, but each represents a particular model of spiritual realisation. The correspondence between the caliphs and the stages does not depend, then, on each one's spiritual rank, but simply means that each of the caliphs manifests the excellence of such and such a stage in the community. It is striking that ʿAlī is the only one for whom the rank of his station and his chronological

---

156. Ibid. fo. 99a. This vision is reminiscent of the image of the six-faced heart of Abū Yazīd al-Bistāmī. See Kubrā, *Les éclosions de la beauté et les parfums de la majesté*, p. 109.
157. *Wāqiʿāt*, fo. 17b.

place in the caliphate correspond perfectly. This comes from the fact that reality is the stage in which, as we have seen, the meaning and the letter are brought together and coincide perfectly. In the same way it is worth noticing that Abū Bakr, in spite of being first chronologically, is seen as conforming to the model of knowledge. These two states are those of the angelic realm, whereas the other two are those of the terrestrial realm. This analysis certainly shows Üftāde's concern to include in his spiritual line the two authorities of ʿAlī and Abū Bakr, in conformity with the brotherhood from which his own way issued, the Bayrāmiyye. From this point of view Abū Bakr occupies a crucial position, for the stage of mystical knowledge corresponds in the order of the subtle centres to the stage of fervent love, as has been mentioned above. Fervent love, says Üftāde, "is the fact that the traveller knows the unification of the necessary with the possible, and by what impulse they are brought into existence. Fervent love is the term which designates this knowledge."[158] Fervent love is in fact none other than the awareness of the relation, indispensable to phenomena, between the created and his creator. Abū Bakr is, then, the model of knowledge of this particular relation, which belongs to the divine order. If this stage, that of the spirit, is one of fervent love, it is a matter of realising the nature of spirit, which "cannot be seen as it is, but is seen when it takes the form of the beloved, and grows in beauty as much as it grows in perfection", so that when it reaches perfection it is seen "in the form of the master".[159] This knowledge, however, can only be truly realised in

158. Ibid. fo. 112b. Abū Bakr is also the model of the traveller of the way of the affirmation of Unity, for he had the habit of putting stones in his mouth so as not to talk, in order to devote himself permanently to invoking the formula of Unity (ibid. fo. 69b). See also the Persian translation of Najm al-dīn Kubrā's *Risāla ilā 'l-hā'im l-khā'if min lawma al-lā'im*, ed. T. Subhānī, Teheran, 1364, p. 18.

159. *Wāqiʿāt*, fos. 71a and 113a, where he also makes clear that the garment that the spirit receives by divine providence is scrupulous devotion. The spirit is a created reality, whose function is to rule over the body, illness signalling its lack of influence, for spirit brings it light, like the sun does to the moon (ibid. fo. 52).

the effacement of the possible before the necessary being, in total annihilation, of which the model is ʿAlī.

Beyond these explanations, the correspondence between the four stages and the first four caliphs, the rightly guided ones, completes Üftāde's doctrine by adding to the hermeneutic of the texts, in the course of the journey through the prophetic degrees of his being, the interior realisation of the succession of the Prophet. This consists of taking on the inheritance of his spiritual heirs. The relationship to the Prophet again appears more central for the Celveti way, insofar as it is not only following a mystical Sufi line but also goes directly back to his most important and closest historical successors, who succeeded him both spiritually and politically. The master thus again underlines the importance he gave to spiritual direction, the function through which the world is reconstituted within the framework of the law, revived by spiritual realisation.

To sum up, we can depict the correspondence between the subtle centres and the perfections in the form of a table:

Law	ʿUmar	Body	Animal	Affection	Secret of lordship
Way	ʿUthmān	Soul	Human	Love	Theophany of divinity
Knowledge	Abū Bakr	Spirit	Angelic	Fervent love	Unveiling of intimate knowledge
Reality	ʿAlī	Secret consciousness	Highest	Amazement	Reality of the divine order

The way of the affirmation of Unity

The Celveti way, Üftāde strongly emphasises, is the way of the affirmation of Unity. "The affirmation of Unity consists of being free of all that is not God, by being His servant."[160] The invocation of this formula occupies the most important place in his way. "The affirmation of Unity possesses a fire and a light. Its fire is negation and its light is affirmation." He explains to his disciple about different uses of this formula: "If you want to banish conscious thoughts, pronounce the negation loudly; otherwise, do the same for the affirmation." Üftāde used both invocation aloud and silent invocation. Invocation aloud, however, is of great importance in his eyes, particularly for beginners.[161] Ismail Hakkı explains that invocation is not done for God, but to combat the soul, which is very hard of hearing, and therefore it is good to do the invocation in a particularly loud voice to make it listen. It is necessary first of all to purify the four subtle centres by negation, in order to afterwards beautify them by the light of affirmation.[162]

> The invocation of the formula of Unity is a tower of strength that has no equivalent in the Names, for it denies the coarseness of the soul and purifies it [...], it is a fortified fortress for those who live in it, and when the seeker enters there, none can take hold of him, and it is the way of the Prophet, as it is the first words that he spoke.[163]

160. Ibid. fo. 15b.
161. Ibid. fo. 4a. Furthermore, Üftāde makes clear that in the Celvetiyye the invocations are practised when standing or sitting, but exclude dance, although he does not condemn it (ibid. fo. 88b).
162. The affirmation of Unity may manifest itself in a white light, as in the vision that Hüdāyī reported to his master, who told him: "The white light is part of the light of the affirmation of Unity, but our aim is the Master of light and the Creator of things" (ibid. fo. 55b).
163. Ibid. fo. 48b.

The power of the formula of the Unity is incomparable for Üftāde. It clearly goes beyond the power of invoking the names, the seven of annihilation and the five of subsistence, which were nonetheless practised in his way.[164] What makes it valuable is both the power of purification, for it includes the negation, and the fact that it is the Prophet's formula. It allows one to follow the Prophet's example and be inscribed in his spiritual line, to follow the four stages which he himself has defined according to a saying which Üftāde attributes to him: "The law is my words, the way my behaviour, knowledge my wealth, and reality the recompense of my state." The doctrine of the four stages thus receives the prophetic guarantee, and leads the master to affirm that "the way that the Prophet and most of the companions travelled was the way of the Celvetiyye".[165] The relationship to the Prophet is also reinforced by the idea that the disciple's invoking of the formula of Unity is not sufficient in itself. In fact the formula pronounced by the disciple is only effective according to his level. Just as the Prophet had a particular invocation that depended on his specific rank, and thus benefited his companions by his spiritual direction, so the disciple should not be content with his own

164. In fact Üftāde is sometimes content to refer to the existence of these names in his teaching, but without actually mentioning the names or explaining how to use them. That is why a succinct overview of these names can only been brought from Üftāde's successors (Yılmaz, *Azīz Mahmūd Hüdāyī ve Celvetiyye tarikatı*, pp. 192–7, with further details in Bahadiroğlu, *Celvetiyye'nin piri Hz. Üftāde ve dīvān'ı*, pp. 208–11). However, in one passage Üftāde refers not to the practical use of the names but their epiphany in the heart. He recommends that his disciple repeat the verse of the Pedestal (*āyat al-kursī*) three times in order to chase away conscious thoughts and to empty his heart of all preoccupation with other than God – in this connection we may remember that Najm al-dīn Kubrā's daily litany (*awrād fathiyya*) begins with the repetition of this verse thirty-three times. Then Üftāde says: "the lights of divinity are revealed, and you contemplate the epiphanies of the most beautiful Names." It is not so much the practice of the names which is important, but rather their epiphany when the heart is completely purified, so that they are a sign of total annihilation: "when the meaning of the words of majesty is revealed, the universe and your existence is annihilated, just as a man who is drowned in water no longer sees anything else" (*Wāqi'āt*, fo. 22b).

invocation. Üftāde summarises this position in a categorical manner: "The aspirant does not reach his aim by invoking the formula of Unity only by himself; it is essential that his master invokes according to his intention, for if the master's invocation is not included in that of the aspirant, the latter cannot reach his aim."[166]

Üftāde also mentions that there are three formulas of Unity:

> The formula of Unity for people like us is *lā ilāha illā Allāh* (There is no divinity other than God); the formula of those who are half-way along the mystical path is *lā ilāha illā Anta* (There is no divinity other than You), because they are at the station of contemplation and they are in need of converse; but the perfect ones hear the formula of Unity spoken by the One whose Unity is affirmed, and it is *lā ilāha illā Anā* (There is no divinity other than Me), because He effaces their existence in the station of total annihilation.[167]

Thus the general formula is one which encompasses the others. It is the practice by which one passes beyond the stages of self-annihilation, and the formula to invoke at the beginning of the path. The two other formulas are stages of this general formula. The second is that of mystics when they are in the middle of their journey, and reach contemplation, and Üftāde mentions it several times in his teaching. It is, he says, "the praise of glory of the prophet Jonah".[168] The last one is no longer pronounced by the mystic, but heard. It corresponds to the agreement by the people of the primordial discourse, when God asked them "Am I not your Lord?" The formula pronounced by the mystic is the response to this question, so that to

165. Ibid. fo. 11a.
166. Ibid. fo. 27b.
167. Ibid. fo. 118a.
168. Ibid. fos. 87a, 106a. This refers to the following passage in the Quran: "And Dhū'l-Nūn [Jonah] – when he went forth enraged and thought that We would have no power over him; then he called out in the darkness: 'There is no God but You. Glory be to You, indeed I have been one of the oppressors'" (Q.21:87).

reach the level of agreement is no other than to return to the source
of all enunciation, and corresponds to the stage where the mystic
loses consciousness of himself before being able to re-descend.[169]
The spiritual journey is also built on the example of the Prophet in
the daily practice of invocation, through the place that the master
holds in the discipline of his disciple. The doctrine of the four stages
implies also other practices, which Üftāde sometimes explains to
his disciple. The disciplines that he advocates are applied essentially
to the first two stages that have to be passed through to reach the
angelic realm. "The traveller in the stage of corporeal nature must
renounce his occupations, be content to eat only what is necessary,
and must cast aside that which has to do with corporeal nature." In
the stage of the soul, "he must beware of the love of possessions and
children, for they are a temptation and lead him to pride".[170] The
aim of the quest being total annihilation, all practices have no other
function than to lead the mystic to his annihilation. The practice
of the formula of Unity leads to the invocation of the heart, whose
fruit is the "place of beautiful return" according to the Quranic ex-
pression. Annihilation later leads to the unveiling of things in their
true reality, but its highest accomplishment is "the vision of God's
beauty".[171]

169. This is certainly the station of the perfect ones, though still incomplete,
for it is not yet the return to creation for the purpose of spiritual direction. That
is the basis for criticising Hallāj's rank, just as Üftāde also did in regard to Nesīmī
(ibid. fo. 23b). Hallāj definitely reached this stage, but he was not able to reach
the station of return, which is why he was not a perfect spiritual director for the
Celvetī master (ibid. fo. 33b).
170. Ibid. fo. 18a.
171. Ibid. fo. 89a.

The heart and the spiritual path

We may ask what the final place of the heart is in this ladder. Alluding to a *hadīth* of the Prophet, Üftāde says that "the heart is the judge (*muftī*) of the traveller: it determines what is necessary for him in his state to be elevated and come close", and he states that "this is only possible through the affirmation of Unity and by the veracity of the words of those people of God who have reached the reality".[172] The affirmation of Unity leads to a total submission, which is the perfection of the creatural condition.[173] In fact, each stage produces peace in the heart, so that the heart passes through these degrees and completes this journey. The invocation of the affirmation of Unity has degrees, by which the heart awakens to its own peace. Divine Unity appears in the heart progressively, insofar as it is severed from each element to which it is attached. When it is emptied of all that is other than God, Üftāde says, the truth of the matter is unveiled. "The affirmation of Unity by the tongue is a door, for the affirmation of Unity in words allows one to reach the affirmation of Unity by spiritual state, and its cornerstone is the peace of the heart." It is a matter, then, of passing from the word to the state, or from the exterior heart to the interior heart, which in itself pronounces the affirmation of Unity when the heart is emptied of that which is other than God.

Thus the heart passes beyond the four stages of the subtle centres, one after the other. This ascension of the heart is an education by which it progresses towards total annihilation.

> In the stage of corporeal nature it is emptied of the attention it devotes towards the delights of nature and desires; in that of the soul, it is emptied of the demands of the soul. As for the spirit and the secret consciousness, they are so pure that the heart in

---

172. Ibid. fo. 92a.
173. Ibid. fo. 102a.

the stage of the secret consciousness pays absolutely no attention to that which is other than God.[174]

The heart is, then, the pilgrim of the subtle centres, the traveller of its own ladder, which unrolls the carpet of the enigma of its being, to reach that which is beyond itself, which is already no longer it but would be nothing without it. Üftāde cites the example of the Prophet to explain this quest, so intimate to the heart that it defines its nature. To pass through each stage, according to Üftāde, "the Prophet asked: 'My God, increase me in knowledge', and the perfect ones asked: 'My God, increase me in bewilderment.'"[175] This bewilderment is that knowledge which culminates in the effacement of the heart to itself throughout the four stages. Üftāde explains to his disciple that there are three kinds of heart: "the heart that flies in the world down here around desires; the heart which flies in the other world around spiritual powers; and the heart which flies to the lotus of the limit around intimacy and prayer. The stage which lies beyond is total effacement and pure annihilation."[176]

The invocation of the heart has a particular quality. "Permanent taste, repose and persistence will only be acquired through the affirmation of Unity by the heart, by emptying the heart of all that is not God." Üftāde describes the power of the affirmation of Unity as the immediate capacity to make all that is not God disappear, in order to remain with Unity. "When the perfect one pronounces *lā ilāha illā 'llāh* once, all that is not God disappears from him and he remains with God. As for me, I do not arrive there in a single time but in three."[177] Thus he underlines the power of the affirmation of Unity, which is the Celveti way, and which allows one at a stroke to reach total annihilation. This is also the stage of reality, whose major characteristic is that it confers tranquillity. We can also understand how this stage is that of reality. This invocation immediately bestows

174. Ibid. fo. 101a.
175. Ibid. fo. 104b.
176. Ibid. fo. 42a.
177. Ibid. fo. 23b.

the realisation of its aim, bringing peace through freedom in regard to all that is not God.

> The heart has an interior and an exterior, in the sense that it has two degrees, one of which is the interior of the other. It is essential to dedicate oneself to the invocation of the formula of Unity by the tongue, until it penetrates the depth (*suwaydā*) of the heart. Once it penetrates it, the work is complete, and if after that the seeker no longer invokes by the tongue, it does him no harm, since from then on it is the tongue of the heart that professes Unity.

For Üftāde the heart is reduced to two parts, one encased in the other. The important point is to reach the bottom of the heart, to purify it so that it proclaims the divine Unity. That is the whole point of invoking the formula of Unity with the tongue, out loud. In its depth the heart also has a specific tongue, such that "when one invokes with the tongue of the heart, this lower world is filled with the formula of Unity."[178] The function of the heart's invocation thus goes far beyond the individual's spiritual quest. The heart through its purification fills the world with its invocation, as if it had become the world itself. Not content with having a hidden tongue, the heart has also two eyes, which allow it to arrive at a certain vision.

> In the same way that man has two eyes in his exterior aspect, he has two eyes in his heart, and if they are open, he contemplates the theophany of attributes. In the same way, they have two pupils, but of extreme fineness. If we content ourselves with saying that they contemplate the theophany of attributes, that is because the theophany of essence can only be contemplated by an intelligible eye, which lies beyond the eye of the heart, and has no pupil.[179]

178. Ibid. fo. 103a. Note that the bottom of the heart is the sixth mountain of the subtle centres according to the Kubrawī Najm-i Rāzī, whose manual of Sufism, *Mirsād al-ʿibād*, was recommended reading by Hüdāyī.

179. The image of the eye with no centre is astonishingly reminiscent of the

The purification of the heart thus results in the vision of the intelligible eye, which is situated beyond itself, in this other place which is like the projection of the heart in pure relation to God.

There comes a moment, however, when the invocation has gone beyond into an even higher station, and it is suspended. When the traveller reaches the station of immersion, beyond the station of invocation,

> there is no more invocation there, for this is the station of effacement, which is that the traveller no longer has any real existence which rises from invocation. The spiritual masters call that "total bewilderment" (*baht kullī*), which belongs to the prophets and to the most perfect of the saints, and consists in the health of the heart and isolation with regard to all that is other than God.

This particular station is also that of fervent love, in which "the lover sees nothing other than love".[180] In this station, where silence of the heart rules, occurs the theophany of essence, the pure vision whose taste never disappears from the consciousness.[181] "The heart which seeks never ceases to turn in every direction, to ascend and to draw nearer, until it has attained the One whose Unity is proclaimed. When it arrives, it is free, and it rests, having cut away all relation with that which is other than God." From then on the heart has reached its purity, "asking nothing more, neither of the earth nor the skies", and has realised the perfect affirmation of Unity.

Üftāde very often compares the heart to the sky: "The heart is like the sky: at times it unveils itself, at other times clouds cover it and it can only be free by rending them and cleaning the dirt in its depths."[182] By being purified of these impurities, the heart becomes

---

image of the circle with no point which characterises the contemplation of the theophany of the Essence according to Najm al-dīn Kubrā (*Les éclosions de la beauté et les parfums de la majesté*, pp. 94–5, 103–5).

180. *Wāqi'āt*, fo. 91b.
181. Ibid. fo. 101b.
182. Ibid. fos. 111a and, for example, 18a.

that "sacred heart", according to the Quranic expression, which extends itself to encompass the four stages of its interior sky. The impurities which are found in it include the demonic realities. The heart is a tablet upon which is inscribed the demon. "The traveller must efface the demon from the tablet of his heart, so that it is clear of the tablets of the specifications of essence and it is free by the grace of God."[183] Because the heart combines in itself the whole of the worlds, the thrones, and the specifications of essence, it must conform to their nature. It is responsible for returning the whole of creation to its creator, purifying it of the impurities that it has taken on. The central position of the heart and its transcendence with regard to the four stages springs from the fact that it has become the created reality of the world, the sky which englobes all the multiple realities. The perfect heart acquires whiteness, which is also the ocean of reality, for it is reality which makes the heart white. "The whitening of the heart is the possession of the prophets, and after them, the perfect ones, and it only occurs after having reached reality."[184] There are also degrees of whiteness of the heart, according to the state characteristic of each person, and these give rise to specific visions. The whiteness of the heart one day appeared to Hūdāyī, as the universe manifested in the form of a huge white cloud. This vision, his master told him, "can only occur through the purity of the heart". The vision of the universe in its whiteness is none other than that of the heart, for "the universe is in the interior of your heart, and not the other way round, since the heart is the largest of all things. Abū Yazīd al Bistāmī said: 'All the universes in comparison to the heart are like a point in relation to an immense desert.'"[185]

The heart is like a tablet, as Üftāde explained above. The heart even contains two tablets which are parts of the two total tablets. These two tablets are the formal tablet and the intelligible tablet. The formal one "contains the 18,000 specifications of essence, and is

183. Ibid. fo. 95b.
184. Ibid. fo. 80a.
185. Ibid. fo. 18b.

susceptible to change and to being reversed [...], whereas the intelligible tablet can neither change nor be reversed. It is not subject to time nor to spatial volume [...] and is to be found in the pre-eternal knowledge of God."[186] The two formal and intelligible tablets, which are present within the heart, are the threshold of these two tablets. The heart of the saint has access to the complete formal tablet, but the second is only unveiled gradually, following total annihilation. In traversing the interior stages of its being, the heart passes beyond the 18,000 specifications of essence which are present in the formal tablet, and attains total annihilation, where it lets the pure divine Unity be by forgetting itself. Then it has a share in the pre-eternal divine knowledge, which is the eternal and immutable 'guarded tablet', which belongs to the divine will. Thus it can bring together again the two dimensions of its being, the reality and the law, by perfecting the corporeal reality, which at the end of its journey flows from the divine existence.

The way of the Unity of Existence

In an unusual passage in the *Wāqiʿāt*, Üftāde describes the ending of the spiritual journey by the well-known term developed by Ibn ʿArabī's successors, *wahdat al-wujūd*, Unity of Existence. The interesting part of this description is that it is not so much a theoretical explanation as the understanding of this doctrine from the point of view of the mystical quest:

> The meaning of the Unity of Existence is that once the traveller has passed beyond the stages of corporeal nature, soul, spirit and secret consciousness, and has annihilated everything, nothing is shown to him other than the One whose existence is necessary. The possibilities are annihilated for him, including his own soul, so that when everything is annihilated, there

186. Ibid. fo. 23a.

remains nothing but the existence of the Necessary Being, which is by Its Own Essence. This is the meaning of the Unity of Existence, and it is not like what people of heresy, who believe in incarnation and unification, think.[187]

This definition refers exclusively to the mystical experience. Üftāde here interprets the Unity of Existence uniquely in terms of annihilation, and takes it to mean union with God, which he calls also the bringing-together again or substantial union, according to the old expression of Hallāj. This definition also allows him to reject interpretations that he considers contrary to the mystic's assimilation of divinity and to the total annihilation of the one who would remove for God the possibility of His Unity being affirmed by the possible things. In fact, for Üftāde, only annihilation as he has defined it – that is to say, the forgetting of self, putting one's self between brackets rather than removing it – allows the realisation of the true doctrine of the Unity of Existence. This is how Üftāde connects his understanding of the mystical journey to the doctrine developed by Ibn ʿArabī's successors. He considers himself one of his heirs, and connects his way to his teaching, which was widely promoted in the Ottoman Empire at the instigation of, among others, the sultans from the beginning of the dynasty. Given that Üftāde insists on the fact that the Celvetiyye is the way of the Prophet and his companions, Ibn ʿArabī's teachings, which represent a Sufism most mindful of law and imperial order, are for him the guarantee of a definite orthodoxy, which was to be maintained throughout the Ottoman Empire.

The spiritual quest of the heart, this aspiration to the Unity of Existence, Üftāde condenses into a prayer, which sums up what guided him throughout his life:

May God grant us pure sincerity in His servanthood, so that we may understand the perfection of His Sovereignty. May He illumine our hearts with the light of mystical knowledge. May

187. Ibid. fo. 109a.

He give life to our existences by the traces of His Unity. May
He render us fit for the happiness of His Union and of His
Vision. Amen.[188]

'Azīz Mahmūd Hüdāyī, orphan since his earliest childhood as he
says himself,[189] was Üftāde's favourite disciple and most important
successor. He followed the same quest in his own lodge in Üsküdar.
He spent a long time following a very strict discipline close to his
master, having little time to go and see his family according to
Ismail Hakkı. A famous anecdote illustrates their relationship, and
allows us a sense of what spiritual life with the master must have
been like in his lodge on the heights of Bursa, and of all the devotion
that Hüdāyī demonstrated towards his master. The story also shows
how Üftāde pointed his disciple to the place where he should base
himself in order to found his own lodge and continue the teaching
of the Celveti way. Every day Hüdāyī was responsible for heating
water for his master's ablutions at dawn. But one day he was late,
and his master got up. He took the jug containing cold water, went
out of the room and held it against his heart, all the while invoking
God. Through his invocation he reheated the water, and went to his
master so that he could make his ablutions. When he poured it out,
Üftāde understood what had happened, and said to him: "My son,
this water has not boiled with fire. Two lions cannot sit at the same
time on the same throne. It is clear that you must now go and settle
down in Üsküdar."[190]

188. Ibid. fo. 15b.
189. This is one of the very rare indications we have regarding Hüdāyī's
childhood, which may shed some light on his reasons for leaving his native
village of Koçhisar in favour of his father's town, Sivrihisar. See Yılmaz, *Azīz
Mahmūd Hüdāyī ve Celvetiyye tarikatı*, pp. 41–2. This is what Hüdāyī himself said
about it: "The master asked me how my father was, and I replied: 'he died seven
days before I was born, and my mother afterwards.' He said to me: 'Then your
condition is comparable to that of the Prophet'" (*Wāqi'āt*, fo. 111a).
190. Hüseyin Vassāf says that this pitcher was made of earth, and that it is
preserved in Hüdāyī's convent in Üsküdar, where he came to settle as ordered by
his master (*Sefīne-i Evliyā*, II, p. 635).

The Poems

The invocation of Hū

Hū[1] keeps on providing the powers of the pilgrim seekers
At each moment a green cushion[2] on which are seated the lovers.

It is constant strength for the gnostics
To pass beyond the way-stations on the path to the Friend.

To say *Hū* with the whole heart and spirit at each moment
Is for the people of sincerity the remedy for their pain.

Hū, which the people of serene purity utter once more,
Will arouse the spirits of those who have arrived.

When the invocation of *Hū* reaches the depths of the heart
The traveller's existence is effaced.

With the uttering of *Hū*, the Reality unveils itself
And thus it is at each moment from His secret for "those who
        remain steadfast".[3]

Üftāde, offer the invocation of *Hū* as a litany
That the traveller may come to know the secret.

Saying Hū

Hū is a dervish's rapture
Hū is a dervish's grandeur

Hū is a dervish's wealth
Uttering *Hū* is a dervish's litany

With *Hū*, one ascends every degree
Saying *Hū* is a dervish's guide

The gates of the way to the Friend appear
Then light surrounds the dervish[4]

When he is liberated from seeing other than Him
The eye of the dervish's heart is opened

Then he will be able to see the beautiful face of the Friend
And the dervish's secret consciousness will be opened up

Üftāde, if you desire the remedy for pain
Serve the dervishes by saying *Hū*.

Oh He and You who is He
(Yā Hū wa yā man Hū)

If you desire the Beloved, my heart,
    Do not cease to pour out lamentations.
Observing His existence, reach annihilation!
    Say "Oh He and You who is He".[5]

Let tears of blood pour from your eyes
    May they emerge hot from the furnace
Say not that He is one of you or one of us
    Say "Oh He and You who is He".

Let love come that you may have a friend
    Your distresses are a torrent
Sweeping you along the way to the Friend
    Say "Oh He and You who is He".

Take yourself up to the heavens
    Meet the angels
And fulfil your desires
    Say "Oh He and You who is He".

Pass beyond the universe, this [unfurled] carpet
    Beyond the pedestal and beyond the throne
That the bringers of good tidings may greet you
    Say "Oh He and You who is He".

Remove your you from you
    Leave behind body and soul
That theophanies may appear
    Say "Oh He and You who is He".

Pass on, without looking aside
    Without your heart pouring forth
        to another
That you may drink the pure waters[6]
    Say "Oh He and You who is He".

If you desire union with the Beloved
    Oh Üftāde! Find your soul
That the Beloved may appear before you
    Say "Oh He and You who is He".

Good tidings arrived the month he was born

The beloved of God[7] is the call to the community
　　The physician at each moment for all those who suffer
The intercessor for this community on the day of resurrection
　　Good tidings arrived the month he was born.

He has illumined the world with light
　　All souls are perfumed with his scent
For this purified one is the beloved of God
　　Good tidings arrived the month he was born.

The king of the excellence of the prophets is Muhammad
　　The beauteous moon of the city of sainthood is Muhammad
The pearl of the ocean of knowledge is Muhammad
　　Good tidings arrived the month he was born.

The sultan on the throne of the law is Ahmad
　　The ocean underlying the sea of the way is Ahmad
The merchant of the pearl of reality is Ahmad
　　Good tidings arrived the month he was born.

The servant whom God loves is Mustafā
　　His existence is for the universe the quintessence of purity
He is the gift to the community from the favour of God
　　Good tidings arrived the month he was born.

Abū Bakr, ʿUmar, ʿUthmān and Haydar[8]
    He made of them guides for the believers
Niche of orientation and pulpit, this is the master of the
        ascension
    Good tidings arrived the month he was born.

The taste and purity of the creatures in the two worlds
        That is the beloved of God and His pure chosen one
            (Mustafā)
For the universe of the heart, it is his light and his clarity
    Good tidings arrived the month he was born.

God said to him "If not for you, if not for you …"[9]
    If you had not been, I would not have created the skies,
That stone and dust could converse with him
    Good tidings arrived the month he was born.

It is he who guides spiritual warriors during the [holy]
        struggle
    He who intercedes for sinners on the day of resurrection
He who causes life to be born in the hearts
    Good tidings arrived the month he was born.

Bless him with benediction and salutation
    Celebrate his birth morning and evening
He is the saintly leader, spirit of the prophets,
    Good tidings arrived the month he was born.

Sustainer of the soul of poor Üftāde
    His resting place is forever union with God
He is the flame that burns in the city of Islam
    Good tidings arrived the month he was born.

You must love

You have to come soon to the Real
    You have to find His wise ones
If you truly cannot find them
    With all your soul and with all your heart,
        you must love.

Those who have loved have found them
    Their souls have reached the Real (God)
Their faith has become whole
    With all your soul and with all your heart,
        you must love.

Always trace out their tracks
    Listen to their beautiful discourse
If you say you would like to see their faces
    With all your soul and with all your heart,
        you must love.

This dervish, this unhappy Üftāde,
    Has become a beggar on the road of God
May God fulfil his desire
    With all your soul and with all your heart,
        you must love.

The way of the Friend

Entrust your soul to the way of the Friend
    If you don't, what else can you do?
If you abandon your soul
    You will surely go with your secret
        consciousness.

Your body and your soul are a burden for you
    Each atom of them bigger than a mountain
If you do not throw down this burden
    You will have a host of troubles to endure.

One has said that the summit is close at hand
    Here is the way to the Friend today
If you leave it until tomorrow
    You will have many ages to wait.

Learn the rule of lovers
    Devote yourself to nothingness
If you reduce your being to non-existence
    You will surely find life everlasting.

Speak of the way of nothingness
    Oh you suffering Üftāde
Whoever takes that road
    Will quickly arrive at the Real.

The call to friends

This is the call to friends to come and realise Unity
    To find the Real's (*hakk*) favour in the realised Unity
That the universes of the heart may be filled with light
    This is the call to friends to come and realise Unity.

His people are those who see the Real God
    Those who rejoin His perfection in the abodes
Those who become again guides for the travellers
    This is the call to friends to come and realise Unity.

Come, let us enter the ocean of realised Unity
    Come, let us see which ways are to be found
There to find the Real God's full satisfaction
    This is the call to friends to come and realise Unity.

Behold what is ever the word of those who know
    The greetings of the Real God reach down to the
        one who invokes
God the Eternal remembers those who invoke Him[10]
    This is the call to friends to come and realise Unity.

The invoker who finds the light of Unity
    Thanks the Real with all his soul and with all his heart
God the Powerful displays His Beauty
    This is the call to friends to come and realise Unity.

His contemplation reaches the station of union
  He devotes his being to unceasing prostration before God
His existence is absorbed in the ocean of light
  This is the call to friends to come and realise Unity.

Such is the wish of poor Üftāde
  May the gracious Name of the Real be the guide
That his knowledge and remembrance be accepted by God
  This is the call to friends to come and realise Unity.

The nightingale's lament

I

At dawn I heard the nightingale lamenting
  Recounting the pain of all those who suffer
Those who heard him took pity and said
  Marvel at this poor nightingale mad with love

I saw that his love-passion had overwhelmed his
    reason
  The rose's serene purity struck deep into his soul
So that he thought it was the remedy for his
    affliction
  Marvel at this poor nightingale mad with love.

The fire of separation had taken over his soul
  He was warbling love-songs in a blaze of passion
Its scent drew him deep into the rose garden
  Marvel at this poor nightingale mad with love.

Under the weight of its perfume he lost his senses
  He lost all control of his body
So that he took on all the burdens of the world
  Marvel at this poor nightingale mad with love.

He searched every corner of the garden
  He could find no roses, neither red nor white
He had lost all hope of union, he knew not when it
    could be
  Marvel at this poor nightingale mad with love.

The rose season passed in this state of anguish
    His soul burnt this time with the flame of
        separation
His drunkenness passed, his cries abated
    Marvel at this poor nightingale mad with love.

Listen well to the words of Üftāde the Nightingale
    That you may trace out the tracks of the people
        of gnosis
If you wish to see the face of the Friend
    Marvel at this poor nightingale mad with love.

II

At dawn I saw where the nightingale had alighted
    He had placed his lantern in the house (*tekke*)
        of the rose
He had drawn his sword to gift his soul to the rose
    Marvel at this poor nightingale mad with love.

He lost his reason until he no longer recognised
    himself
    His reason in ruins until he recovers from his
        rose anguish
Never will those who are lovers of God perish
    Marvel at this poor nightingale mad with love.

The hue of the rose paled, it lost its bloom
    Its scent no longer reached the nightingale
No-one came any more to the rose garden
    Marvel at this poor nightingale mad with love.

Then reason returned to the nightingale's mind
   Unable to see the rose, wherever he looked
Aflame with the fire of separation, he went forth
   Marvel at this poor nightingale mad with love.

Traversing land and sea in this anguish
   Enduring such torment and pain
The thought of the rose's perfume gnawed away
      at his heart
   Marvel at this poor nightingale mad with love.

One man of God said: leave the ephemeral rose
   Did you not know it was perishable since
         pre-eternity?
No good can come out of a transient beauty
   Marvel at this poor nightingale mad with love.

Such is the supplication of poor Üftāde
   May the gift of God reach his soul
May His light and His clarity fill the hearts
   Marvel at this poor nightingale mad with love.

III

At dawn I heard the nightingale lament
   The scent of the rose had intoxicated his soul
He had lost himself, he knew not where
   Marvel at this poor nightingale mad with love.

Blood mixed with tears flowed from his eyes
   His soul had foundered in the perfumed scent of
      the rose
He had forgotten his exterior and his interior world
   Marvel at this poor nightingale mad with love.

Those who saw him pitied this poor sufferer
   He flew in the sky vigilant, sleepless
The rose had reduced his soul to slavery
   Marvel at this poor nightingale mad with love.

Unless his soul is able to rejoin the beloved
   And for his pain are found a thousand kinds of remedy
This separated soul will never reach that land
   Marvel at this poor nightingale mad with love.

Plunged in the perfume of the rose, his existence
     disappeared
   Renouncing the rose, he prostrated himself
     before God
Such is the eternal contemplation of lovers
   Marvel at this poor nightingale mad with love.

Now the rose became the nightingale's lover
   She cried: "Oh sincere nightingale mad with love
May God make you deserving of His beauty"
   Marvel at this poor nightingale mad with love.

These words are the nightingale of Üftāde's soul
   What he calls rose garden is the country of union
It is the hand of Divine Power which leads the lovers
   Marvel at this poor nightingale mad with love.

IV

At dawn I saw the nightingale's bed
    He had set up his tent in the shade of a rose
Wish for him to give up his soul and his possessions
    Marvel at this poor nightingale mad with love.

He collapses drunk from the perfume of the rose
    The fire of separation fills his head through and
        through
The ocean of the heart boils and overflows
    Marvel at this poor nightingale mad with love.

Sometimes he weeps, sometimes he makes up verses
    Sometimes taken with madness he cracks his head
        against stones
Sometimes he crosses mountains, and winters in the
        wilderness[11]
    Marvel at this poor nightingale mad with love.

Sometimes he rests in silence, staring at nothing
    His heart, forever bound to the rose, does not
        open towards another
He enters into retreat and never comes out
    Marvel at this poor nightingale mad with love.

He plunges himself into the pangs of torment
    He doesn't know what he is
His only desire is to see the face of the Friend
    Marvel at this poor nightingale mad with love.

He imagines that with that picture in mind he can
      reach union
   Laying his heart in shreds and tatters
Obviously he has never met a person who reached
      that spiritual state
   Marvel at this poor nightingale mad with love

Listen to the words of Üftāde, the nightingale
   Efface your intimate being in the scent of the rose
If you should really wish to see the face of the Friend
   Marvel at this poor nightingale mad with love.

V

At dawn I heard the nightingale lamenting
   Indulgently singing tender gazels
Branding the souls of the lovers who heard him
   Marvel at this poor nightingale mad with love.

I said: "Oh nightingale mad with love and
      wonderment
   How many times will you cry and call?
To reach reunion is not possible in this state"
   Marvel at this poor nightingale mad with love.

Put aside these songs and verses
   Listen to what has been said by the pure
      elected one
From white and black withdraw your existence
   Marvel at this poor nightingale mad with love.

Take the celestial Buraq[12] to the country of
    annihilation
  If you wish no separation to stay in your soul
Then you will reach the refuge of the people
    of Unity
  Marvel at this poor nightingale mad with love.

In that abode neither body nor spirit may be
    discerned
  There neither sea nor ocean to be contemplated
There is the remedy for the pain of lovers
  Marvel at this poor nightingale mad with love.

There is there neither plaintiff nor plaint
  There is found neither desire nor inclination
There no mention made of lowest or highest
  Marvel at this poor nightingale mad with love.

Such is the word of poor Üftāde
  No-one can see this station
So long as he has not reached the peace and blessing
    of God
  Marvel at this poor nightingale mad with love.

VI

At night I saw the nightingale of dawn
  Flying high in the station of union
The meanings opened up and he spelt them out
  Marvel at this poor nightingale mad with love.

I said: "Oh nightingale mad with love
    You deserve to reach that abode
You who were sincere in the way of your beloved"
    Marvel at this poor nightingale mad with love.

There remained in him no strength to reply
    He knew there neither separation nor union
Such is the final destination of lovers
    Marvel at this poor nightingale mad with love.

It was from annihilation that nothingness struck the
        nightingale
    He could see nothing other, be it white or black
None but the Creator knew his state
    Marvel at this poor nightingale mad with love.

His existence sank in the ocean of reality
    His prostration grew and grew in perfection
Thus is the eternal contemplation of lovers
    Marvel at this poor nightingale mad with love.

When the nightingale is aloft, reality is his spirit
    They are neither in the mountains nor in the nest
There is neither stone nor thorn in this sphere
    Marvel at this poor nightingale mad with love.

These words do not apply to poor Üftāde
    He does nothing but trace out the tracks of the
        gnostics
May God give him eyes to witness
    Marvel at this nightingale, falcon in the land of
        the Friend!

The nightingale's praise

At dawn the nightingale began a hymn of praise
He wished his work to be lauding the rose.

He sang of the rose's perfection till morning
And his soul drowned in the scent of the rose.

He said to the rose: "Grant me the favour of
    union with you
So that on the way I may sacrifice my soul."

She replied: "Do not cut off your neck for that
    which is nothing
My scent will vanish, my colour fade and
    become dust."

Purify your heart, liberate it from all that is
    other than God
That the skies may never be a veil for you.

You must renounce your inclination to colour
    and perfume
Wear again the soft robe of indigence.

Such is the prayer of poor Üftāde
That the heart may not sin nor contemplate
    any other [but God].

May tidings come

Oh my dear friends, give me tidings of this sublime Lord
Be generous, give me tidings of this august Master.

There was a time when I knew Him
There even appeared to my spirit an address from the sublime
    Master.

Now that I am in this world of bodies, I have fallen into separation
Night and day I am consumed with longing to quit this present
    state.

May I reach a higher state and rejoin the Master
Oh Friend! May I draw nearer to Your abode and leave this lower
    world.

May I find the satisfaction of God, the clarity of His Beauty
And drown my existence in the Light and traverse the most
    Beautiful Names.[13]

May my meditation reach Unity and may It always be my
    invocation
In each breath may I lose myself and pass beyond both high and
    low.

May the benevolence of the Real arrive and disclose the secret of
    "Glory be to Me"[14]
May tidings come to Üftāde's spirit when hearing the One who is
    Named.

Let us love the Real God

Come friends, let us find there today the taste of faith
May the compassion of God come, that we may take human form.

Let us follow the way with care and attention; let us remain
    standing day and night
That He who veils may accept us, heaping upon us His generosity.

With all our spirit let us love the Real God, remaining firm on His
    path
That upon our spirits He may arise, to share with us Knowledge.

Let us banish from our hearts all other than Him, that God may
    pour out His providence
To be at peace with regard to all other and that the Real may grant
    us His favour.

May our spirit become knowing with the knowledge of Reality
And may we reach the station of union, going beyond all the worlds
    of existence.

My existence was effaced by plunging into the ocean of Reality
May this journey find completion in the station of annihilation in
    God.

The desire of poor Üftāde is to taste the vision of Beauty
May the Master be munificent to all lovers by His generosity.

May God grant us guidance

Oh friends, I have dreamt of my country
    From whence I came, I have known
My route came from the heart
    May God grant us guidance.

The heart, that is His door
    If it opens, your spirit is joyous
Before ever your body becomes earth
    May God grant us guidance.

Go! Take then this road
    Catch up with those who follow the way
Give up on all that exists in the world
    May God grant us guidance.

Rejoin those who have attained
    Those who have arrived at reality
Those who have abandoned their heart
        to God
    May God grant us guidance.

May you grow wings and fly
    Traverse the seven seas
And choose well between good and bad
    May God grant us guidance.

May the return journey be completed
   May the heart find its goal
May it be with friends in this knowledge
   May God grant us guidance.

Poor, miserable Üftāde
   His heart wounded by exile
Wandering homeless in this world
   May God grant us guidance.

May God grant right direction

Day and night let us lament and cry
    May God Most Forgiving grant right direction
He is the Guide for us as for the people of gnosis
    May God Most Forgiving grant right direction.

With all our heart let us fervently love God
    Let us be sincere towards God in the way
Render us worthy of seeing His beauty
    May God Most Forgiving grant right direction.

Through generosity may He bring us to the house
      of His Majesty
    Making us all ascend the degrees to Perfection
Rendering our eyes worthy of His Beauty
    May God Most Forgiving grant right direction.

Meeting up with the prophets and saints
    Meeting them and kissing their hand
May we all reach the unveiling of His Beauty
    May God Most Forgiving grant right direction.

May the path of His Beauty reach serene purity
    May the bestowal of the Real be ever greater
May the permanence of the Real be revealed
    May God Most Forgiving grant right direction.

Through His satisfaction may He let us partake of
the feast
That with the banishing of separation all shall
find peace
May He say: "Your satisfaction is all that I want"
May God Most Forgiving grant right direction.

May the beloved of God intercede for poor Üftāde!
May this be his portion prescribed by God
For he is the doctor for the soul in separation
May God Most Forgiving grant right direction.

May He grant us the grace of His Beauty

Let us follow God's order
    In our heart let us invoke
In our heart again let us meditate
    That He grant us the grace of His Beauty.

Let us always say Allāh
    With our whole heart say Ah!
May God bestow upon us His Generosity
    Granting us the grace of His Beauty.

May the field of the heart be opened wide
    May we see Reality's light
May we taste the wine of His fervent love
    Granting us the grace of His Beauty.

May nothing other be shown
    May all sufferings be cured
May all meanings be opened up
    Granting us the grace of His Beauty.

May subsistence be constant
    May the heart be firm in contemplation
May it be sheltered from torment
    Granting us the grace of His Beauty.

Diving into the ocean of reality
  Finding the hidden treasure full of gems
May the heart reach union
  Granting us the grace of His Beauty.

May poor Üftāde's meditation
  Be always invocation of Him
Be entirely gratitude to Him
  Granting us the grace of His Beauty.

Let us apply ourselves this day

Oh my friends! Let us apply ourselves this day to thinking
    most assiduously about God
That by His providence God does not cast us
    into the fire.

May the soul be granted victory
    over corporeal nature
May His love cause the rain of generosity to pour down
    on our spirit.

May the spirits reach the rose garden, which is union
    with the Beloved
That plunging into the ocean of light they re-emerge
    upon the shore.[15]

May the spirit of the prophets appear on the crest
    of this ocean
Seated upon thrones of light,[16] gazing upon each other

Then at that moment all the sincere ones shall find
    the lovers
And see the beauty of the Friend, remaining forever in
    that state.

May permission to look be granted to the heart,
    that it may begin
To flow throughout these luminous lands, clearing
    the road to God.

Your name is Üftāde, oh dervish, turn summer and
    winter towards God
May God bestow His providential care, grasping
    the hands that fall.

From my origin was I separated

Oh my friends say nothing to me! From my origin was I separated
Leaving my homeland – from my origin was I separated.

With friends I shared taste, with lovers desire
To this world they sent me – from my origin was I separated.

"Love of your native land is part of faith", said the Envoy, may he
    aid us!
To this he alludes: from my origin was I separated.

His way they showed, they told me where to go
I could not find the strength! What now? From my origin was
    I separated.

Heedlessness has overcome me, I cannot find my King
How shall I go, and where? From my origin was I separated.

Leaving my origin and all my existence, I re-kindled hope
From God I await munificence – from my origin was I separated.

Poor unhappy Üftāde, in exile I have remained. Help me!
Have pity on me, oh One and Only Refuge – from my origin was
    I separated.

Free yourself of saying "I"

What wonder it would be to know the remedy for my pain
Which is the king who rules over the 18,000 worlds![17]

Closer to me than myself, the One who veils me
Consumes me with the fire of distress, He who from view
    remains hidden.

He who renders me mad, ransacking my heart and depriving
    me of reason
Acting upon my secret consciousness, He is the beloved soul
    of my soul.

It is idleness without doubt to abandon oneself to suffering
Imprisoned, having lost the way, the doors tightly shut.

Whoever exhales his last breath before death takes him
Lives by offering his spirit in sacrifice to the way of God.

Behold first what you seek, to arrive at your goal
One who frees his interior and his exterior from separation
    is truly Man.

Oh you suffering Üftāde! Free yourself of saying "I"
For whoever says "I" remains an animal, in separation.

Shall I ever find the One?

Will there ever be a day when I shall see the One I adore?
Through lamentation shall I ever find the One who is
    my goal?

Day and night crossing the fire of separation through union
    with You
At each instant yearning, shall I ever find the One who was
    promised me?

Your union has always been the remedy for my pain
Healing my wounds, shall I ever find the One who is my
    beloved?

The day will come when touching the earth I see the world
    of the Real
Plunging into light, shall I ever see the One who is my
    deepest desire?

Day and night uttering sighs and cries of distress
Shall I be ever united to this Marvel I complain to?

What will happen to this servant if he cannot see his King?
Freeing me of veils, shall I ever see the One I invoke?

Oh, do not look at the blackness of poor Üftāde's face
Day and night dreaming, will I ever see the One I adore?

Will I reach the light?

What a strange day! Will I reach the light of His Beauty?
If my soul listens to His Word, will I reach the mountain
    of Union?

Contemplating His sweet Beauty, like a moth flying towards
    the candle
Burning my wings and my feathers, will I fall into the fire of
    His Love?

Day and night my heart and soul dwell on God without
    ceasing
If my soul becomes one, will I reach the Master of my heart?

If the heart drowns in the way of His Beauty
If Reality is unveiled, will I reach His secrets?

If I reduce the realm of my existence to nothing before dying
That with the souls of the dead it be gathered, will I reach the
    source of Union?

If I cross the seven oceans and drink the water of life
In the marketplace of union, will I get to the caravanserai of
    the One?

What can this poor Üftāde do about such weakness?
May Ahmad's light come to the aid of this indigent one's soul.

Tell me, where is the way to the country of the Friend?

Lovers of the country of the Friend
    Sincere ones on the path of God
Skilled with those who suffer
    Tell me, where is the way that leads
        to the country of the Friend?

Pain has cauterised my heart
    Blood has rained from my eyes
My soul has obstructed my road
    Tell me, where is the way that leads
        to the country of the Friend?

Patience and resolution, I have none left
    Union with Him my soul has not
        found
His Beauty my eyes have not seen
    Tell me, where is the way that leads
        to the country of the Friend?

My way led me to a dwelling
    Where my hand was struck with
        impotence
In separation came my death
    Tell me, where is the way that leads
        to the country of the Friend?

One day I shall come close to a perfect one
   I will ask him the way to the Friend
I will follow his way with devotion
    Tell me, where is the way that leads
       to the country of the Friend?

In spiritual taste may He
    Strengthen poor and miserable Üftāde
His tongue will utter these words till the
      day he dies
    Tell me, where is the way that leads
       to the country of the Friend?

Guide us to the country of the Friend

Those who seek the way of God
    Sincerely devoted to His Beauty
Those who desire reunion with Him
    Guide us to the country of the Friend!

They sent me here
    Where I lament today as yesterday
Whoever I find, I ask about Him
    Guide us to the country of the Friend!

Oh prophets! Oh saints!
    Oh devoted ones! Oh pure ones!
Oh dervish, initiate of annihilation!
    Guide us to the country of the Friend!

Earths, heavens!
    Mountains, stones!
Waters, winds!
    Guide us to the country of the Friend!

Paradise and grace
    All the flashing-eyed beauties and
        cup-bearers of Paradise
All those who witness His existence
    Guide us to the country of the Friend!

You people of knowledge who act so well
    You people of piety who behave with such
        virtue
You people of poverty, content with what you
    have
    Guide us to the country of the Friend!

The whole universe is a path that leads to Him
    We must traverse it from beginning to end
Until the roads reach a clear destination
    Guide us to the country of the Friend!

Poor and unhappy Üftāde
    Oh One and Only! Oh Single One!
        Oh Unique One!
May Your Favour bring aid
    Guide us to the country of the Friend!

Give me tidings of the Friend

You sages of Truth
   Lords of the land of the Friend
Guides of those who seek
   Give me tidings of the Friend!

Into my heart separation has come
   From my Friend have I been sent away
Never will I be able to prepare myself
   Give me tidings of the Friend!

I have remained in exile
   I am full of pain and unhappiness
I have sunk into much anguish
   Give me tidings of the Friend!

One who cannot find Him
   His soul will never know joy
May He strip me of me
   Give me tidings of the Friend!

Through Him may I find Him
   Leaving body and soul behind
May the Rich beyond need open up
     the way quickly
   Give me tidings of the Friend!

May I be raised up to His Union
    And contemplate His Beauty
I will tell him all my weaknesses
    Give me tidings of the Friend!

Poor and indigent Üftāde
    Covered in wounds inside and out
Never abandon this unhappy one
    Give me tidings of the Friend!

The only remedy for separation

I

Union is the only remedy for separation
Those who do not attain Union cannot be at peace

Oh my God, grant me the gift of Your Union
That in my heart Your Union may take over

The whole universe is hoping for all kinds of favour
The desire of the lover is always for Union

The lover's heart is afflicted by separateness
Let it rejoice in Your Union, You who give relief
    and aid!

Union is the alchemy of separation
Let separation be transformed into Union,
    Oh You who give strength and solidity!

May the veil of this revelation be lifted from
    the eyes
May it be effaced and expelled,
    Oh You who give light and clarity!

Gladden this miserable Üftāde with Favour
    and Generosity
Take pity on him, lead him to Union,
    Oh You who give relief and aid!

II

Union is the only remedy for separation
Those who do not attain Union cannot be at peace.

Oh my God, grant me the gift of Your Union
Make of our hearts the lair of Your love.

The whole universe is hoping for all kinds of favours
The desire of the lover is You, You, indisputably.

The lover's heart is afflicted by separateness
Let it rejoice in Your Union, in the gardens of paradise.

Union is the alchemy of separation
Let there be sometime a chance to reach Union.

May all that is other be effaced and expelled
So that in this circle there remains neither body nor soul.

Open up the heart of unhappy Üftāde
By Your Grace and Favour, to his faith add vision!

The fasting moon has returned

Make the call, call the lovers
   The fasting moon has returned
Churning up the ocean of compassion
   She has filled up the universes again.

She whom God speaks of in the Quran
   Whom the prophets all loved
Whom God gave the community
   The fasting moon has returned.

She who has power over all the months
   The remedy for those who suffer
The right action God sent us
   The fasting moon has returned.

She who brings gifts from the Friend
   Who clears away all darkness and
       oppression
Who gives birth to knowledge in the
     spirits[18]
   The fasting moon has returned.

She is Power for seekers
   Glory for gnostics
Paradise for believers
   The fasting moon has returned.

Light to the hearts
  Joy to the believers
Crowds to the mosques
  The fasting moon has returned.

Üftāde's soul loves her
  Ever praising this month of fasting
So journey to the country of the Friend
  The fasting moon has returned.

We have reached the fasting moon

All thanks to God, my friends!
    We have reached the fasting moon
She is true guidance for the believer
    We have reached the fasting moon.

She clears away all sins
    and you are born anew
She brings you back to the country of
      the Friend
    We have reached the fasting moon.

We have seen the beautiful crescent
    They have rejoiced at her approach
They have given thanks to God
    We have reached the fasting moon.

Our hope lies in God the Rich
    That He show us His Beauty
Let us address our praise to God
    We have reached the fasting moon.

Out of devotion for His beloved,
    God has given to us the fasting moon
And we have seen God's favour
    We have reached the fasting moon.

To miserable Üftāde, Oh Lord,
    And all the people of faith
Grant the light of fasting
    We have reached the fasting moon.

The value of fasting

This is the call to the believer: come!
    Let him follow the tradition of the fasting
        prayer (*terāvīh*)[19]
Let him learn the value of fasting
    If from God he wants beauty.

Let him always submit to adoration
    Let him be upright all night long
Let him fast in the daytime
    If from God he wants beauty.

The goal is His Beauty
    Which is outspread within the Quran
Let lovers rejoice at this
    If from God they want beauty.

Fasting is the way to His Beauty
    When you reach His Perfection
Observe well the origin and destination
    If from God you want beauty.

Observe the customs of fasting
    All your faults will be pardoned
Pass your days with the prayer beads (*tesbīh*)
    If from God you want beauty.

Miserable Üftāde's pain
    This litany of desiring Your Beauty
His pain is to wait on the road
    If from God he wants beauty.

The fasting moon has gone again

Oh my friends, let us cry
    The fasting moon has gone again
Let us lament, let us grieve
    The fasting moon has gone again.

A light from God she came
    Her light filled the skies
Taking the sincere ones by the hand
    The fasting moon has gone again.

The ways of the unjust and their hands,
    She just severed them
Struck down their cities
    The fasting moon has gone again.

To the soul she gave purity
    To the pact she was faithful
For the pain she gave healing
    The fasting moon has gone again.

She gives savour to fasting prayers
    Causes lamps to shine forth
Gives glory to mosques
    The fasting moon has gone again.

She is the influx from God
    She is manifest to lovers
Filling their hearts with light
    The fasting moon has gone again.

She fills Üftāde with joy
    Awakens the remembrance of believers
Brings freedom from worries
    The fasting moon has gone again.

May we one day be His

Oh lover! Oh sincere one!
    Come, let us go to the side of the
        Friend
To see the beauty of the Beloved
    May we one day be His.

All the envoys and prophets
    At once lovers and standard-bearers
To carry the remedy for those who
        suffer
    May we one day be His.

That for people it be law
    That love fall on the hearts
That they may see the beauty of the
        Beloved
    May we one day be His.

In His Book He has promised
    Brought good tidings to the lovers
Opened the way to His Beauty
    May we one day be His.

For lovers there is union
    For believers closeness
For sincere ones glory
    May we one day be His.

Those who have reached the land of the
    Friend
  Their language perpetual invocation
From God come their tidings
    May we one day be His.

Üftāde has fallen into separation
    God will guide him to union
And to glory with the believers
    May we one day be His.

One with the One

Oh lover! Oh sincere one!
　　If it is tidings you desire
Look upon the One who is in the city
　　　　of existence
　　Pay no attention to other.

Until you see wonders within yourself
　　You must find the real goal
In a deep sea you must dive
　　There, where you cannot see the shore.

You must be one with the One
　　You must be existent with Existence
You must not stay with others
　　Nor find any sign of them.

From every shore comes the call:[20]
　　"Oh you who search for Me, I am God"
Turn your gaze to the side of His Beauty.
　　There is no other journey for you.

Oh Üftāde! He whom you seek for yourself
　　Gives Himself constantly, from beginning
　　　　to end
All remains united to Him
　　That is the tidings that come from Reality.

One drop

You, my heart, you are not separated
   From union with your Beloved, you!
How can you complain
   At each breath of separation from Him?

Who does your Beloved love?
   When you hear this, you start lamenting
Then you lament all the time
   That is what is pleasing to Him.

Forever I am exposed, veil-less
   From me the me was lifted off
That day I arrived giddy with drunkenness
   To drink the wine of Unity.

Those who drink the wine of Unity
   May they be called to come
Entering the desert of Unity
   They shall taste the pure water of the Friend.

Why this sadness, Üftāde? Enough for you
   This union with the Beloved
One drop of Unity was offered you
   Out of His grace and His gift.

In my rose garden

Since Your love bathed my heart
    Stripping away my name and distinctions
It overflowed and into the exterior poured out
    Tidings of the secret hidden within me.

As He robbed me of myself
    He lifted the veil from my soul
At once it turned into the poetry of fervent love
    Which the body of my soul recited.

That which I wished for myself,
    Was close to me: the One who manifests
        Himself by Himself
Why then these sobs and complaints?
    From my loving Friend comes that which
        is mine.

That which no eye has ever seen
    Words have never explained
Faces which never passed through the heart
    Have shown themselves in my rose garden.

If you were perplexed like me
    If you were in love from head to toe
You would have no name, no fame
    Knowing the most Beautiful Names.

If only every lover like me
    Were sincerely following Your way
Be he ascetic or libertine
    Had he heard what my tongue utters.

I am the trader in musk
    I have discovered the treasure-house of gems
I have plunged into the ocean of reality
    Let the purchaser do his buying at my store!

What is this pain which affects you, oh Üftāde?
    Union with the Beloved has come
One drop of Unity has been granted you
    Out of His grace and His gift.

Cure this pain

My God, I desire of You Union
    Be graceful, show us Your Beauty
The fire of separation from You scorches us
    Be generous, oh Merciful One,
                Cure this pain, Master! Help us!

Make yourself worthy of the fire of separation, my soul
    The fire of these flames is nothing
Man is too feeble and cannot find satisfaction
    Be generous, oh Merciful One,
                Cure this pain, Master! Help us!

The doctors have found no remedy for this pain
    From You alone comes the cure for this ailment
Be generous, Oh my King! Glory to You!
    Be generous, oh Merciful One,
                Cure this pain, Master! Help us!

Poor me! From my country I fell into exile
    Feeble that I am, my hands fall from weakness
Yet these words continue to flow from my tongue
    Be generous, oh Merciful One,
                Cure this pain, Master! Help us!

Oh Üftāde! If you desire to be one with the Beloved
    Cast the cup of dignity and modesty to the ground
Nurse your wound in the fire of separation
    Be generous, oh Merciful One,
                Cure this pain, Master! Help us!

The secret hidden within

My heart, if you desire tidings of the secret hidden within you
Lift the veil from your face and turn your gaze to no other
    [than God].

Having reached the lordly effusion, let the light of God come
Let the veil of the Beloved be seen, then you will find His signs.

May you reach this life which is found by drinking the water
    of life
Go beyond existence, saying: "Here death is no longer".

Oh heart, the light of the Beloved gives you so much largeness
That all creatures have found eternal abode within you.

May anxiety no longer invade your heart, Oh Üftāde
For it has reached its goal, hearing the echo.

Come close

Come close, oh You who lay the foundations in the city of
    my heart
He who bends the necks of 18,000 worlds to His order.

Night and day my liver is roasted in the flame of fervent love
He who makes a Farhād[21] of my existence by shattering the
    mountains.

The fire of affliction has so burnt my heart it has reduced it
    to cinders
He who always beats in my heart by means of taste.

This lover's eyes are entirely consumed by a stream of tears
He who lays the foundations of His love by filling him with
    wonderment

From night till dawn he pours out sighs of lamentation
"Until he merits Him" says He who directs my heart.

Time after time He addresses the lovers with His call
    [to prayer]
That is His promise, He who through ardent desire
    makes them eternal.

Such is Üftāde's object of desire for all eternity
The One who rejoices our hearts by displaying His
    loveliness and beauty.

Even closer

Again my heart has met the candle of the Beloved's beauty
Lifting the nuptial veil from His face, it has plunged into His
    lights.

How many years of waiting, saying it would see Him –
Then all of a sudden His theophany, and it rejoined its Beloved.

Tasting wine from Unity's cup, which the hand of the Beloved
        held out to it
It was as if suspended by the mysteries of the secret of "I am the
    Real" (*anā 'l-ḥaqq*).[22]

When it knew the meaning of "two bow-lengths", it understood
That it had not been fooled, then it attained His "or even closer".[23]

Üftāde! Truly, in this heart there is anxiety no longer
In finding the object of the quest, it has reached its Master.

Let me hear Your Beautiful Name

If I cannot see Your Beauty
    Let me hear Your beautiful Name
If I cannot be united to You
    Let me hear Your beautiful Name

One day to see Your beauty
    To contemplate Your perfection
To reach union with You
    Let me hear Your beautiful Name

Being united to You through ardent desire
    Seeing Your Beauty through taste
Being with all the lovers
    Let me hear Your beautiful Name

Your beautiful Name is our guide
    Your Love is also our delight
All of Your Names are our heart's recitation
    Let me hear Your beautiful Name

In whichever language Your Name is
        mentioned
    Let Your thought reach the heart
That it may always show You gratitude
    Let me hear Your beautiful Name

The heart shall find His theophany
    The true satisfaction of the Real God
And the serenity of His Beauty
    Let me hear Your beautiful Name

Such is the way of Üftāde
    To the way of God he has said "yes indeed!"
That his heart always invokes
    Let me hear Your beautiful Name

Do not drive us away from Your door

Oh my Beloved, how shall I find You?
    How will I see Your beauty?
How can I one day reach Your union?
    Do not drive us away from Your door.

Your pain always burns me
    My heart always melts for you
Existence always ruins me
    Do not drive us away from Your door.

May Your love reach down to my soul
    May it give strength to my faith
May life reach the body that is mine
    Do not drive us away from Your door.

May our hands gain in power
    May our tongues invoke
May our ways satisfy You
    Do not drive us away from Your door.

May we travel up to Your essence
    May my faith gain in strength
May my travelling be in virtue (*ihsān*)
    Do not drive us away from Your door.

We have found You in the interior
   Leaving body and soul behind
Oh You, the Rich who pours out Grace
   Do not drive us away from Your door.

Such is the pain of Üftāde!
   May he be effaced in Your light
That is his soul's purity
   Do not drive us away from Your door.

Come closer

I

Come closer, oh You who march through the city of my heart
You who always make lovers drunk and senseless.

You who remove me from separation, sending me forth on
    these paths
You who have built the form of man out of four elements.

You who always desire me, sending me tidings of You
Driving me along in this passion, naked, burnt.

You who are beyond all place, You who have no place
Where can one find You, You who have withdrawn?

Seeing You fills my heart with suffering
Who would go to see You, if it were not You who alleviates
    suffering?

Do not content Yourself with showering Your mercy upon
    lovers with red roses
You who by the veil of lights bring forth their laughter.

Come Üftāde, if you desire to reach Union! You who suffer
Efface your being, for the only one who has being is the One
    who lives forever.

II

Come closer, oh You who pace round the courtyard of my heart
You who through fervent love make an infinite ocean of one drop
    as small as an atom.

As You cannot be contained in 18,000 worlds, through this love
You make of the world a prison, sending it tidings of You.

By once giving the savour of Your discourse to be tasted by my soul
You make me fall in the world, You who make me lament and cry.

My existence is for me the barrier which obstructs Your path with
    its atoms
Take my hand, free me from this obstacle, You who grant grace
    and favours.

The people of gnosis have said: As long as you do not leave this
    place
You will not know the One who keeps Himself concealed.

As long as you have not reached Mecca and gone into retreat
You will not see the One who sets your secret consciousness in
    motion.

If you want to know, Üftāde, then look at your secret consciousness
Then you will know who is the One who walks there.

III

Come closer, oh You who lay the foundations in the city of my
heart
You who bend the necks of 18,000 worlds to Your order.

You who remove me from Your closeness, returning me to these
confines
You who rejoice my heart with the promise of a tomorrow.

You who make me mad by stealing my heart and capturing my
reason
You who make a Farhād of me by reducing the mountains of my
existence to dust.

When Your secret becomes visible, for the lovers, it is like day
You who by veiling Your light lead them on the way.

To contemplate Your Beauty the lovers must be worthy
You awaken their remembrance by opening the eyes of their
spirit.

Let Üftāde's heart guide him with fervent love
You who with Your love provide for the souls of the lovers.

IV

Come closer, oh You who heal the wounds of my heart
From pre-eternity You have made my heart sick with love of You.

Your union is the remedy for the pain of lovers
You who give to fervent lovers the strength to see Your Beauty!

Had Your Beauty not been promised to lovers
Who would fortify the lover who laments?

It is Your invocation which causes the souls to moan
You who cause light to drown the souls in invocation.

It is they who have seen the light of Your Beauty in the mirror
It is they who have understood who it is that annihilates and
        gives existence.

Entrails streaming, eyes full of tears, liver shot through and
        through
It is You who bring the lovers into the 18,000 worlds.

Oh suffering Üftāde, this is your vow forever
Abandon your heart to the Beloved who brings forth things into
        the open.

What ails you?

I

What ails you, my heart? Have you a peerless beloved?
Have you a sovereign who rules over the 18,000 worlds?

His Beauty will never be unveiled to the lover as long as he
    does not die
Have you then a soul like Ismāʿīl, prepared for sacrifice?

Day and night you aspire to throw yourself into the fire
Have you then a wondrous body like Abraham, that burns not
    in fire?

With one glance, He annihilates the being of all the universes
Have you then a hidden secret consciousness to perceive this
    Beauty?

Oh my heart! You are always hoping to rejoin the original nest
Have you then wings and feathers created by the Holy Spirit?

Why are you trying to get there? I wish I understood
Have you then a beloved within your bosom that is woven
    from the bodily palace?

How strange to have used such symbols, oh Üftāde!
Have you then signs within you that you have reached God's
    light?

II

What ails you, my heart? Have you a peerless beloved?
Have you no other occupation than to carry on wailing and
    complaining?

With each breath you try to throw yourself into the fire of fervent
    love
Do you possess such a body that does not burn in the fire, like that
    of God's intimate friend?

You are always saying you want to surrender your soul
Do you possess such a wondrous soul, like the spirit of Ismāʿīl?

Eyes streaming, entrails streaming, liver shot through and through
Do you possess such patience moulded by trial, like Job?

Head for the country of the Beloved, pass by all that which is other
Do you possess such a light that passes from the Holy Spirit to your
    eye?

You pass your days and nights spying on the beauty of the Beloved
Do you possess such a light that flows from Ahmad's secret to your
    eye?

How strange you dare to utter these words, oh Üftāde!
Do you possess such signs within you that you have reached God's
    light?

III

What ails you now, my heart? Did you remember your origin?
You cried out in pain, recalling your separation.

Did your soul at that moment hear tidings of the people of gnosis?
It is for that that you moan about your fate day and night.

Is it the country of the Beloved or just a scent of it that has brushed
    your spirit?
Enduring the thorn of the world below, you have pined for the
    garden of roses.

Has a glance from the Beloved shot forth into your secret
    consciousness
That you were reduced to nothing, shattering the helmet of the
    head and soul?

Or has a flash from Beauty's gleam touched you
That by divulging your secret, you made your place dark?

If there has appeared from the light of Unity a light
Then know, oh you who suffer, that you have acted well.

Do not utter these words, oh suffering Üftāde!
You will deeply distress those who have reached this spiritual state.

Surrender your spirit

Since I understood the symbols of lovers, I have lost my patience
   and repose
Closing my eyes to that which is other [than God], my soul has
   regained repose.

Since I solved the riddle of Your separation, Union became my
   desire
My hand is impotent, what can I do but send forth sighs and
   lamentations?

Perhaps one day He will take pity on this servant who implores
   Him
Come closer! You who suffer, relieve your soul.

As long as you do not surrender your spirit, vision is not possible
From pre-eternity such a choice has been given to the lover.

If you surrender your spirit, I will open up your inner eye
If you pass through the veils, your pain will be healed.

If you desire your Beloved, oh suffering Üftāde!
Efface your being, proclaim nothingness.

The one who knows his origin

The one who knows his origin cannot live in these places
Like him, the heart flees far from what is other than God.

The heart that remembers its origin in these places
At once Love comes galloping into its abode.

Finding his aim, reaching the object of his adoration
Freeing himself from separation, realising union.

He reduces his being to nothing, he leaves not a trace of his
     existence
Existence is a veil barring realisation of union.

Whoever brings his own being into this abode
Even though he search day and night, will find nothing.

The perfect master is drowned in the light of the affirmation
     of Unity
He gives relief to the seekers, bringing out manifold treasures.

Throw your drop into the ocean, oh suffering Üftāde!
Let it be the ocean, full of countless sorrows!

Through Your invocation

Oh my God, grant the heart illumination through Your
    invocation
Displaying Your sweet Beauty in the affirmation of Unity,
    oh God!

Guide Your invocation as the means to Your Essence
Those who attained always attained through invocation.

Give our souls eternal life through Your invocation
That by invocation the one who is saved from annihilation
    finds true existence.

May His beauty be displayed to the eyes, may the lights of the
    Essence be revealed!
In light drown Your lovers, oh God!

That which silence grants them is the promise of His Beauty
For Him they always sing grace and praise.

They are hoping today to see Your sweet Beauty
From beginning to end they have no other desire.

Free yourself from all otherness, oh suffering Üftāde!
That in rejoining the light of His Beauty you find serenity.

There is no other remedy

You are the remedy for my ill, there is no other remedy
To regard any other than You is a fault in the lover.

They do not consider their pain, nor hope for a cure
Their aim is You alone, oh Generous Master of gifts!

They want no other to come into their thoughts
To see Beauty is for them cure for their wounds.

Were they to become masters of all 18,000 worlds,
Not an atom would satisfy them, if they were separated
from Your Beauty.

Remove your heart from all otherness, oh suffering Üftāde!
Let the call of the Unseen reach the ear of your soul.

The remedy for my affliction

The remedy for my affliction is You – my Exalted King, come
    to my aid!
The dearest soul of my soul is You – my Exalted King, come
    to my aid!

From his homeland cast into exile, ah! the fire of separation has
    consumed him
Grant me total union with You – my Exalted King, come to
    my aid!

To put one foot on Your way is beyond my power
Take my hand, free me from this malady – my Exalted King,
    come to my aid!

In the fire of separation the liver roasted, entirely burnt up
I no longer have strength to burn – my Exalted King, come to
    my aid!

By the exile of prophets, by the honour of saints
By the heart of all lovers – my Exalted King, come to my aid!

If for one instant You cast Your regard upon the 18,000 worlds
All would reach their aim – my Exalted King, come to my aid!

This is the constant wish of suffering Üftāde!
He aspires to see Your sweet Beauty – my Exalted King, come
    to my aid!

Surrender to invocation

Whoever madly desires to see the Beauty of the Friend, let him
Surrender himself to invocation
Whoever wishes, like the moth, to dissolve in the candle, let him
Surrender himself to invocation.

The way which leads to the Beauty of the Friend is the invocation
Of those who invoke
Whoever aims to reach the light of this Beauty, let him
Surrender himself to invocation.

Whoever is sincere in the way of God must
Give up his soul
Whoever is fit to give up his soul let him
Surrender himself to invocation.

Whoever invokes with all his spirit and with all his heart will reach
The One he invokes
Whoever is reduced to nothing in invocation, let him
Surrender himself to invocation.

Whoever aspires to be invoking God, with every breath
Let him implore.
Whoever ardently desires to truly find the King, let him
Surrender himself to invocation.

This is the constant wish of
Suffering Üftāde!
That he who contemplates the Friend, renouncing all other, let him
Surrender himself to invocation.

Come let us invoke the Real

You who love the Essence of God
   Come let us invoke the Real
Let your sighs rise up to heaven
   Come let us invoke the Real.

Let us go to His rose garden
   Let us follow the invocation of the Real
Let us see what there is in your heart
   Come let us invoke the Real.

Let the ways open from the heart
   Let the Real God pour out His compassion
Let us drink the wine of the river Kevser[24]
   Come let us invoke the Real.

The path lies in invoking the Real
   The tongue is for invoking the Beloved's
        company
Such is the state of lovers
   Come let us invoke the Real.

It is the sign of His beauty
   The way of the prophets
The secret of the saints
   Come let us invoke the Real.

He who names Me without ceasing
   Without ceasing I remember him[25]
So his soul is united with Me
   Come let us invoke the Real.

Poor Üftāde's sadness
   If his litany is permanent invocation
By invocation arrive those who arrive
   Come let us invoke the Real.

Let us invoke the Real on this day

All thanks to God, my friends
    Let us invoke the Real on this day.

We said Allāh so beautifully
    It flowed so easily from our tongues
That the King gave assent to it
    Let us invoke the Real on this day.

Look what came from our hands
    Constant proclamation of Unity
Drawing from the heart His name
    Let us invoke the Real on this day.

Those who invoke the Creator
    Those whom God loves
Are joined with the angels
    Let us invoke the Real on this day.

Ever we hope from God
    That His light penetrate our hearts
To be the pointer to His Beauty
    Let us invoke the Real on this day.

Oh you dervish Üftāde!
    May the doors of generosity open
May all meanings be discerned
    Let us invoke the Real on this day.

Let Your lovers see

Manifest the light of Your Beauty
    Let Your lovers be filled with desire
Sever their hearts from all other
    Let Your lovers be filled with taste

Draw back the veil that covers their eyes
    Drown them in Your lights
Show them the way to Your Beauty
    Let Your lovers be resolved.

Drown them in the sea that embraces all
    Release their souls into the ocean
Plunging into that high sea
    Let Your lovers inhale Your perfume.

How wondrous the one who can see
    Your Beauty, my Lord
For it is You again who know Yourself
    Let Your lovers have patience.

The mountains are still thirsting for
      Your light
    Those who burn are effaced
Consumed, reduced to ashes
    Let Your lovers go on yearning.

The veil which hides Your Beauty
    Is the dervishes' own being
Strip them of their being
    Let Your lovers find annihilation.

All desire of You only You
    Üftāde's soul hopes for this
That You grant us Your Feet[26]
    Let Your lovers see Your Face.

If you yearn

While you can proceed safe and sound
  Be always ready to serve
Dedicate yourself utterly to the invocation of God
  If you yearn for the beauty of the Real.

Dedicate yourself to the five prayers
  Without concern for summer or winter
And reach the object of your supplication
  If you yearn for the beauty of the Friend.

Continue to fast throughout the year
  And purify your existence
Prostrate yourself before God
  If you yearn for the beauty of the Friend.

If you have strength, perform the pilgrimage
  Take the route of the desert and go
Remove from your heart all your own intentions
  If you yearn for the beauty of the Friend.

Sigh with longing for the town of Medina
  Look out for the light of the Prophet
Follow his way (*sunna*)
  If you yearn for the beauty of the Friend.

Follow your road, Üftāde!
  This day let your tongue invoke
And lift up your hands in prayer
  If you yearn for the beauty of the Friend.

An incurable pain

As I walked in my own condition
    I encountered an incurable pain
Travelling through my country and my city
    I encountered an incurable pain.

All that I knew faltered, confused
    My union collapsed into separation
All my friends deserted me
    I encountered an incurable pain.

When my path brought me to the throne
    When I came to the high places
When I was joined with the angels
    I encountered an incurable pain

So many sighs did I let forth
    I reduced all existence to nothing
To see the Beloved my only hope
    I encountered an incurable pain.

To make my reason understand
    None of my thoughts could manage
This is my tongue's invocation
    I encountered an incurable pain.

All the gnostics I questioned
    Does anyone understand my pain?
I found none gave me answer
    I encountered an incurable pain.

Poor Üftāde, this pain
    Better to keep it hidden in your heart
From yourself will you get the reply
    I encountered an incurable pain.

No other wish

My God take me for Your beloved
  For I have no other love but You
How am I to reach You?
  I do nothing but wrong.

My heart remembers "Glory be to Me"
  Eyes drenched with tears of blood
I have laid down my head and my soul in
      this path,
  I had no choice.

Here am I once again, back in this dwelling
  Immersed in the ocean of contrition
In a dream I met sweet love's apparition like
      a zephyr
  I have lost all repose.

I am neither dervish living in detachment,
  Nor crown nor throne of government
In this transient house of exile am I exiled,
  I have no other home.

Black is my sinner's face, poor destitute Üftāde
  Fire I kindled, and to remain beside the fire
      I have no other wish.

Let me . . .

Oh my God! Do not leave me where I have fallen, pick me up!
 I cry on and on, just for one moment
  Let me laugh.

For the love of rejoining You, I have given my whole existence
 I am poor, without resource
  Let me be filled with Your Light.

Oh my King! At this moment when You invite me
 Reveal Yourself in Your Essence
  Let me be killed.

You Lord are the source of generosity, oh Generous and
  Merciful One!
 In the sea of compassion and forgiveness
  Let me be cast.

I am Üftāde who walks in the ocean of wonder, oh Beloved
 May my time here be successful
  Let me be brought to Your Union.

The state of the dervish

Alas for my poor existence thus passed!
    What a beautiful reign has been the state of the dervish

Enter as dervish with cloak and crown
    There is no reproach in what I say
Come, be a dervish – I won't force you
    What a beautiful reign is the state of the dervish.

When dervishes find clothing, they rend it
    Drinking the wine of love until their thirst is slaked
That is how it was for Abū Bakr and ʿAlī
    What a beautiful reign is the state of the dervish.

A dervish puts sandals on his feet
    In Paradise he walks swaying
God knows the state of each dervish
    What a beautiful reign is the state of the dervish.

Had we known the true value of dervishes
    We would have frequented them night and day
Seeking our Master, we would have found Him
    What a beautiful reign is the state of the dervish.

One such dervish was Bayezīd Bistāmī
    In the dervish state did he find remedy for his pain
While Ibrāhīm Edhem[27] surrendered his crown and his
        throne
    What a beautiful reign is the state of the dervish.

NOTES TO THE POEMS

1. *Hū* or *Huwa* signifies "He", designating God, and is used in the ritual invocations in a large number of orders, especially the Celvetiyye, for whom it is part of more advanced invocations.
2. Allusion to the green cushion on which the Prophet mounted at the time of his assumption.
3. Quranic term.
4. Alluding to the experience of perceiving lights during the invocation, which shows the influence of the theory of coloured photisms, which was developed by the Kubrawī way, on the Celvetī order following Üftāde's teaching. These colours vary as and when the traveller ascends the ladder of the subtle centres: black for nature, red for the soul, yellow for the spirit, and white for the secret consciousness (Bahadiroğlu, *Celvetiyye'nin piri Hz. Üftāde ve dīvān'ı*, p. 212).
5. This formula of invocation became part of that of the Pole of Poles: *Ya Hū wa ya Man Hū lā ilāha illā hū* (ibid. p. 210).
6. In reference to Q.XXV.48: "He it is who sends the winds as heralds of His Mercy, and we send down from heaven pure water."
7. The beloved of God is the name given to the Prophet Muhammad.
8. This refers to the first four caliphs, Abū Bakr, 'Umar, 'Uthmān and 'Alī ibn Abī Tālib, who correspond to the four stages of the Celveti way (see Introduction).
9. Hadīth: "If not for you, I would not have created the world."
10. Allusion to the verse: "Invoke Me and I shall invoke you; thank Me and do not be ungrateful to Me" (Q.II.152).
11. This wilderness may also connote the spiritual world.
12. The Burāq is the name of Muhammad's winged horse, upon which he was carried during his assumption. The poem alludes to the spiritual ascension of the mystic.
13. This alludes to the epiphany of the Names, which is reached by total annihilation (see Introduction).
14. Alluding to the ecstatic paradox of Bistāmī, the mystic most often

mentioned by Üftāde in his teaching: "Glory to Me! Glory to Me! How sublime is My rank!"

15. Alluding to the return to the created world for spiritual direction after total annihilation. Without this return the spiritual journey is incomplete.

16. Reminiscent of the image in the *hadith qudsī*: "Those who love one another in My Majesty shall have a raised dais of light which will be the envy of prophets and martyrs." (Quoted in Ibn 'Arabī's *Mishkāt al-anwār*, 33: see S. Hirtenstein and M. Notcutt, *Divine Sayings*, Oxford, 2004, p. 50.)

17. The theme of the 18,000 worlds recurs several times in the *Wāqi'āt*. This number corresponds to the 18,000 interior stages of the heart, for each of which there is a specific unveiling and a health accorded to the heart, so that in traversing all the worlds the heart gains perfect unveiling and health (*Wāqi'āt*, fo. 88a). This is also the 18,000 specifications of the essence, within each of which there is a prophet, and the saint can only pass through each one through the intercession of the Prophet Muhammad. It is only when returning from this journey through the 18,000 universes that the saint receives sainthood. Lastly, it is the 18,000 thrones present in human existence (ibid. fos 18a–b).

18. Abstinence is the condition for the revelation of knowledge. Najm al-dīn Kubrā also stresses this point, quoting a saying attributed to Jesus in his commentary on the Quran.

19. This refers to the special practice of *salāt al-tarāwīh*, the long series of supererogatory evening prayers which are performed during Ramadan.

20. The hearing of a call from every side is an effect on the spirit by the name *Hayy* (the Living One), the fifth of the names of annihilation, according to Üftāde (*Wāqi'āt*, fo. 121b).

21. Farhād is the name of the lover of Shīrīn, wife of Khusrev-Perviz, who was the last Sassanian ruler before the Arabs overran the Persian Empire. The theme of Farhād and Shīrīn has become famous in Iranian literature through Firdawsī (d.1020 or 1025) and Nezāmī (d.1209).

22. The famous ecstatic paradox of Hallāj.

23. Quotations taken from the Quran (L.III.9).

24. Kevser, or Kawthar in Arabic, is usually taken to refer to a river in Paradise which the Prophet saw near the climax of his ascension. At the foot of a tree, so vast as to give shelter and shade to the whole

Islamic community, there were two rivers: the river of Mercy (*rahma*) and Kawthar. After bathing in Mercy, Muhammad was able to cross Kawthar and enter Paradise. According to its esoteric interpretation, Kawthar represents the vision of unity in multiplicity (*kathra*, from the same root as *kawthar*) and multiplicity in unity.

25. This passage alludes to the verse: "Invoke Me, and I invoke you; thank Me and do not be ungrateful to Me" (Q.II.152).

26. Allusion to the Two Feet of God, which rest upon the Footstool/Pedestal (*kursī*), representing the two principles of Mercy and Wrath. The Feet lie below the Throne upon which is seated the All-compassionate (*Rahmān*).

27. Ibrāhīm Edhem (or b. Adham, AD 730–77) was a prominent Sufi of Balkh in Khurasan, who was well known for having renounced his kingdom in favour of the spiritual path. He is here contrasted with Bayezīd Bistāmī (d. AD 874), who appears to have always been poor.

BIBLIOGRAPHY

Claude Addas, *Ibn ʿArabī et le voyage sans retour*, Paris, 1996.

Ibn ʿArabī, *The Seven Days of the Heart*, Oxford, 2000.

Ibn ʿArabī, *Wird*, Oxford, 1979.

Mustafa Bahadıroğlu, *Celvetiyye'nin piri Hz. Üftāde ve dīvān'ı*, Bursa, 1995.

Irène Beldiceanu Steinherr, *Scheich Üftāde der Bergründer des Ğelvetie Ordens*, Munich, 1961.

Ismail Hakkı Bursevī, *Kitābü'n-netice*, Istanbul, 1997.

Ismail Hakkı Bursevī, *Kitāb-i silsile-yi shaykh-i Ismāʿīl Haqqī bi-tarīq-i Jalwatiyya*, Istanbul, 1291.

Ismail Hakkı Bursevī, *Rūh al-Mathnawī*, Istanbul, 1287.

Ismail Hakkı Bursevī, *Sharh al-usūl al-ʿashara*, Istanbul, 1256.

Ismail Hakkı Bursevī, *Üç Tuhfe: Seyr-i Süluk*, Istanbul, 2000.

W. Chittick, *The Sufi Path of Knowledge*, Albany, NY, 1989.

M. Chodkiewicz, *Le sceau des saints*, Paris, 1986.

M. Chodkiewicz, *Un océan sans rivage*, Paris, 1992.

H. Corbin, *Avicenne et le récit visionnaire*, Teheran, 1954.

Yunūs Emre dīvānı, ed. Mustafa Tatcı, Istanbul, 1998.

Kudsi Ergüner, *La fontaine de la separation*, Paris, 2000.

G. Gobillot, *Le livre de la profondeur des choses*, Lille, 1996.

G. Gobillot and P. Ballanfat, "Le coeur et la vie spirituelle chez les mystiques musulmans", in *Connaissance des religions*, Jan–Sept 1999 (57, 58, 59).

S. Hirtenstein, *The Unlimited Mercifier*, Oxford, 1999.

Azīz Mahmūd Hüdāyī, *Ālemin yaratılışı ve Hz. Muhammed'in Zuhürū*, Istanbul, 1997.

Azīz Mahmūd Hüdāyī, *Ilim-Amel: Seyr u Süluk*, Istanbul, 1988.

Azīz Mahmūd Hüdāyī, *Waqiʿāt-i Üftāde*, MS Hacı Selim Ağa 249.

Mahmūd Cemāleddin el-Hulvī, *Lemezāt-i Hulviyye*, Istanbul, 1993.

Mustafa Kara, *Bursa'da Tarikatlar ve Tekkeler*, Bursa, 1993.

Mustafa Kara, *Tekkeler ve zaviyeler*, Istanbul, 1980.

Fuad Köprülü, *Türk Edebyatı'nda Ilk Mutasavvıflar*, Ankara, 1984, 5th edn.

N. Kubrā / N. Rāzī, *'Ayn al-hayāt*, MS Halet Efendi 18.

N. Kubrā, *Awrād fathiyya*, MS Şazelī 106/4.

N. Kubrā, *Les éclosions de la beauté et les parfums de la majesté*, Nîmes, 2001.

N. Kubrā, *Risāla ilā'l-hā'im l-khā'if min lawma al-lā'im*, Teheran, 1364.

Menākib-ı Üftāde, ed. A Yünal, Bursa, 1996.

Ahmet Yaşar Ocak, "Oppositions au soufisme dans l'empire ottoman aux quinzièmes et seizièmes siècles", in *Islamic Mysticism Contested*, Leiden, 1999.

Reşat Öngören, *Osmanlılar'da Tasavvuf: Anadolu'da Sūfiler Devlet ve Ulemā (XVI Yüzyıl)*, Istanbul, 2000.

Rūzbehān, *L'ennuagement du coeur*, Paris, 1998.

Rūzbehān, *L'itinéraire des esprits*, Paris, 2000.

Sijistānī, *Chihil majlis*, Teheran, 1366.

Somuncu Baba, *Tühfetü'l ihvan*, Istanbul, 1977.

Mehmed Şemseddin, *Yādigār-ı şemsī*, ed. M. Kara and K. Atlansoy, Bursa, 1997.

Ziver Tezveren, *Seyyid Azīz Mahmūd Hüdāyī Dīvānı*, Istanbul, 1985.

Mehmed Üftāde, *Dīvān-i Üftāde*, ed. Bursalı Tahir Efendi, Istanbul, 1328/1910.

Mehmed Üftāde, *Üftāde Dīvānı*, Bursa, 2000.

H. Vassāf, *Sefîne-i Evliyā*, Istanbul, 1999.

Hasan Kāmil Yılmaz, *Azīz Mahmūd Hüdāyī ve Celvetiyye tarikatı*, Istanbul, 1982.